DATE DUE

AUG 27 1998	APR 2 - 1999
SEP 1 2 1998	APR 2 6 2000
OCT 3 - 1998	DEC 0 9 2000
OCT 1 5 1998	
OCT 3 0 1998	APR 9 - 2001
NOV 1 4 1998	SEP 2 3 2001
Dec. 01, 1998	FEB 1 4 2004
DEC 26 1998	
JAN 1 1 1999	MAR 1 3 2004
JAN 3 1 1999	
FEB 2 2	MAY 2 9 2007
	OCT 1 0 2007
MAR 9 - 1999	

THE PRESENCE

OF ABSENCE

THE PRESENCE
OF ABSENCE

ON PRAYERS AND AN EPIPHANY

DORIS GRUMBACH

BEACON PRESS ▪ BOSTON

BEACON PRESS
25 Beacon Street
Boston, Massachusetts 02108–2892
www.beacon.org

BEACON PRESS BOOKS
are published under the auspices of
the Unitarian Universalist Association of Congregations.

03 02 01 00 99 98   8 7 6 5 4 3 2 1

This book is printed on recycled acid-free paper that contains
at least 20 percent postconsumer waste and meets the uncoated paper ANSI/NISO
specifications for permanence as revised in 1992.

Text design by Anne Chalmers
Composition by Wilsted & Taylor Publishing Services

Library of Congress Cataloging-in-Publication Data

Grumbach, Doris.
The presence of absence : on prayers and an epiphany / Doris
Grumbach.
p. cm.
Includes bibliographical references.
ISBN 0-8070-7084-X (alk. paper)
1. Prayer—Christianity.   2. Spiritual life—Christianity.
I. Title.
BV215.G78   1998
248.3'2—DC21   97-52256

I AM GRATEFUL TO

Walter Dickhaut
Daniel Harvey
Edward Kessler
Ellen LeConte
Paul Munson
Allan Sandlin
Margaret Whalen
Barbara Wheeler
and Esther Williston

all of whom, in one way
or another, contributed
books, ideas, quotations,
challenges, disagreements,
and useful, relevant material
to this book.

The truth is that every sheet of blank paper by its very emptiness affirms that nothing is as beautiful as what does not exist. In the magic mirror of its white expanse the soul beholds the setting where signs and lines will bring forth miracles. This presence of absence both spurs on and, at the same time, paralyzes the pen's commitment. There is in all beauty an absolute that forbids our touching it—it sends forth something sacred that gives pause and strikes the man about to act with doubt and awe.

—Paul Valéry, "La Feuille Blanche"
written for *La Feuille*

CONTENTS

SINGLE FILE

As a young camper in the Catskill Mountains, raised on the strict cement of New York City streets, I remember the summer pleasure of walking through the woods on a very narrow path, so small that I had to put one foot in front of the other to go forward. "Single file," we were told to walk. It meant walking one by one; but I thought it described one foot at a time, an emphasis on the smallest possible approach to progress.

Sixty-seven years later, I see that I am now trying to walk an inner life in idiosyncratic single file. It may well be that *via trita est tutissima*—the beaten path is the safest—but I have meandered from it and taken the *via singulatim*, a road of my own, in my attempt to reach what I have been searching for all these years.

I offer this rather elaborate image to clarify what it is I shall not, cannot, do in these pages. I cannot prescribe this journey, this route, this search, for anyone else. I believe that such treks into the interior must be made alone. The single track must be limited to one traveler. Its map will not be useful to any other person.

What is difficult about the trip is its extent. Dag Hammarskjöld reported in his surprising, posthumously published *Markings*, describing his secret spiritual life, that "the longest journey is the journey inward."

For some years I have looked at guidebooks, "how-to" books, personal accounts, advice-to-the-prayer-life works, all offering helpful hints on attempting the same expedition. They are well intentioned, I am sure. But they violate the one rule of which I am certain: no one can act as guide for anyone else. No one way is better, or best. All travelers must pack their own baggage, start out alone, travel single file, endure all the disappointments, despairs, and darknesses by themselves, and be resigned to making very slow progress. Still, as Montaigne said, "It is not the arrival but the journey that matters."

With this disclaimer, I shall try to describe my long and continuing search to recover a sense of the presence of God. The Quaker writer Thomas Kelly (of whom you will hear a great deal more later) thought that the most fundamental thing his writing could do was "bring people into the presence of God and leave them there." Of course, I cannot hope to accomplish his first action, when I have not yet found the way there for myself. So I will settle for writing an account of a journey that continues, and to leave the reader there, to embark upon his own stormy sea.

AS IT WAS IN
THE BEGINNING

And in our sleep
pain, which can not forget
falls drop by drop
upon the heart
until in our own despair
against our will comes wisdom
by the awful grace of God.

—Aeschylus

THE EXPERIENCE OF PRESENCE

Many years ago an extraordinary thing happened to me. I have never been able to forget it. I have tried to believe it did not happen. But the memory of it, nagging, persistent, unavoidable, has never left me. For more than fifty years I waited for it to happen in the same intensity again. That it did not I attributed to the overcrowded condition of my life, and to my unworthiness.

It was a simple thing: two years after the end of World War Two, I sat on the shallow steps of a small house we owned in a village, Millwood, in Putnam County, a little north of New York City. My husband had taken our two, very young children in our wondrous new Ford to the market in Chappaqua, a nearby town. I was alone, for me a rare condition. I do not remember thinking about anything in particular in that hour except perhaps how pleasant, in my noisy life, how agreeable, the silence was.

What happened was this: sitting there, almost squatting on those wooden steps, listening to the quiet, I was filled with a unique feeling of peace, an impression so intense that it seemed to expand into ineffable *joy*, a huge *delight*. (Even then I realized the hyperbole of these words but I could not escape them.) It went on, second after second, so pervasive that it seemed to fill my entire body. I relaxed into it, luxuriated in it. Then with no warning, and surely without preparation or expectation, I knew what it was: for the seconds it lasted I felt, with a certainty I cannot account for, a sense of the presence of God.

You cannot know how extraordinary this was unless you understand that I was a young woman without a history of belief, without a formal religion or any faith at all. My philosophical bent was Marxist; I subscribed to the "opium-of-the-people" theory. I had never read the account of Julian of Norwich's "shewings"; I had never heard of Simone Weil and her experience in Assisi. For me to have been visited by what Monica Furlong in *Travelling In* has described, in even greater hyperbole, as "a spiritual radiance, a marvelous bliss, a noble freedom, an ecstatic sweetness . . . an overflowing abundance of immense delight" was incomprehensible. But more astonishing to me, at that moment, was that I identified, without a moment's doubt, Whose presence it was I was experiencing. I cannot account for this certainty; I only know I was sure.

Then, after those long seconds, I felt an ebbing, a leaking out from me, a sense of increasing loss of the mysterious Substance around me, above me. The resultant feeling of emptiness was enormous, and strange to me. All my life (twenty-seven years) I had been filled with ideas, memories, fears, thoughts about everything I had experienced: memorized sentences from books, scraps of music I loved, visions of pictures I cherished. The space that was my mind was never without bits and pieces of content. This emptiness was inexplicable to me.

Until those inexpressible moments I had taken no notice of God. I had given His existence no attention, except to harbor a thoughtless conviction that God could not, reasonably, exist. When the sense of His presence had passed, my reason returned in the form of questions I asked myself until my family returned. But I went on for a long time mulling over the questions: How did

I know who It was? Why did I so unhesitatingly give It the name of God? What did I need to do to get Him back?

I have read other accounts of such an experience, the most compelling by Simone Weil, a French philosopher and scholar of the classics. In 1937 at the age of twenty-eight (she writes in her *Spiritual Autobiography*, a long letter to her Dominican friend Father Perrin) she spent "two marvelous days at Assisi":

> There, alone in the little twelfth-century Romanesque chapel of Santa Marie degli Angeli, an incomparable marvel of purity where St. Francis used to pray, something stronger than I was compelled me for the first time in my life to go down on my knees.

Simone Weil was an unbelieving, socialist child of Jewish parentage who had no preparation for such a moment. She had read no mystical works and had never prayed: "I had never said any words to God. . . . I had never pronounced a liturgical prayer." Her life, until that moment of mystical compulsion to kneel, had been filled with every kind of affliction: terrible, almost constant migraine headaches, sinus infections, bodily pain, and voluntary hunger and self-deprivation in order to share the poverty of her fellow workers in factories and the hardships of war.

Still, "it" happened to her, as it did to me, the sense of an inexplicable visitation by an unseen, unknown Presence.

I think it was then, or soon after, that I went to church. I hoped that, in a hallowed place, and with the help of Holy Rite, I might again experience a moment of "noble freedom," the least of Furlong's seemingly exaggerated phrases.

It never happened again, at least not with the same force, with never the same astonishing sense of epiphany. For almost fifty years I continued to pray in community. In all the welter of ceremony and rite, the daily office and the Eucharist, I would not encounter that overpowering sense of Presence. It never happened, to my great regret, almost to my grief, in any of the "regular" places and during the regular practice of corporate prayer.

APOLOGIA

Dear Allan: I have been afflicted with a kind of spiritual inanition. Church attendance has become for me an arid, sterile affair, more duty and obligation than reward. I have become aware that while my mouth was active in church, my spirit remained somnambulant.

For some months I have been reading about the experience of contemplative prayer, a practice to pursue alone. You will say, with some truth, that I am indulging my old, well-known preference for solitude and silence, my regrettable dislike of all social and communal activities and now this is extended to prayer. I have to take this observation seriously, but still, not being able to find any sense of God in community, even at the communion rail, I must try some other place, some other way. In the newsletter which came in this morning's mail you write, "Perhaps during Lent . . . we could look forward for just a few brief moments simply to be." And then you suggest some activities for "simply being": praying, reading, dancing, singing. And you end with, "Or perhaps to sit with a friend and talk about nothing of consequence, or to be quiet together."

I was struck by the last phrase, because it seems to contain an impossible condition. How often, do you suppose, two persons

sitting together have been quiet? For me, *simply being* has begun
to be a condition of the mind that precludes togetherness. Solitude is an essential condition, without the distractions or restric-
tive unisons of corporate prayer (these words are Thomas Merton's), for the way I am trying to learn to pray.

In another newsletter I read a message from the "publicity"
chairman of the church: "It is time to come together, as often as
we are able, to prepare for the celebration of the Resurrection." It
ends with an exclamatory "I'll see you in Church!" Corporate
celebration will always happen, of course. But for me it is no
longer a fruitful occasion.

I wondered if one could celebrate alone, if those words contra-
dicted each other. Perhaps it is necessary to be with others in order to celebrate: the word, the dictionary tells me, means to "per-
form publicly ... to honor with rites," and the celebrant is
described as the "officiating priest." I, in my needy egoism,
wished to seem to be the celebrant, in a sense, to celebrate by
praying alone.

I hope you will understand and excuse my absence. My respect
and affection for you as my rector is very great. My sympathy for
you is even greater: a charismatic, loving man whose spiritual
life must be severely tried, almost consumed, by your duties as a
church CEO, a leader, somewhat like a stage manager, responsible for the determination of the liturgy for an ever growing congregation, responsible for fidelity to the rubrics. Perforce, you are
a sincere believer in the often onerous role you have been trained
for and ordained to. How much easier it is to be the person in the
pew, responsible only for the integrity of one's own prayer, but
often, unhappily, having to concentrate on keeping step with
unison responses and adjurations.

Too often now I find the *business* of church keeps me from the real enterprise of prayer. While there is still time, I must be about the journey I have started on. I hope you will understand and forgive.

PLACE

Most of the faithful give evidence of their belief in public places. For them, worship is a communal act carried out in a consecrated or holy place where ceremony is predetermined, and the actions and postures of the body—kneeling, bowing, standing, making symbolic signs—are prescribed, almost automatic, so many times in a lifetime have they been performed. For many, they provide the warm security of unquestioned repetition, for others the outward demonstration of inner conviction.

Worship often begins in small gatherings. These inevitably expand to require governing bodies which, of necessity, must lead a worldly financial life at some distance from the worshiper in the pew. Religious institutions, now solidified and hierarchic, justify their existence in many ways. The most persuasive justification I have come upon is Peter L. Berger's. In *A Far Glory* he holds that "it is the very purpose of any religious tradition [for these words I read "institution" or "formally established body of worship"] to preserve for generations of ordinary people not only the memory of the great founding events but the possibility of replicating them in a much lower key." In another place he writes that "religious experience would remain a highly fugitive phenomenon were it not preserved in an institution. Only the institutionalization of religion allows its transmission from one generation to another."

Thus, for Berger, religious institutions are needed as repositories for the unique experiences of their founders, mystics, and saints. The past is one of the strong reasons for the existence of church, church place, and church governance. Another, of course, is the solidification and continuation of all matters of dogma. Simone Weil writes in *Spiritual Autobiography:*

> A collective body [the church] is the guardian of dogma; and dogma is an object of contemplation for love, faith, and intelligence, three strictly individual faculties.

Since this is true, she reasons, the individual will be ill at ease in church; these faculties cannot be exercised, I take her to mean, in a social, corporate setting. She says, in the same letter, "What frightens me is the Church as a social structure."

My daughter, Barbara Wheeler, president of a Presbyterian seminary, listened to me on a long dark drive through the country, and then countered my view of the failure of public worship (for me) in a letter. "Faith," she wrote, "entails a response—specifically, that the love of God prompts us to show others what that love is like."

I accepted this, but not the absolute necessity of it. For someone like me, faith is not linear, a display, moving from the individual into the world beyond; but rather circular and centering, revolving around the hope of a hungry soul to meet up with God, for reunion with Him at some fortunate time. In old age, time and energy being limited, there seems no longer a need to display to others what the search for the sense of God is like. Church attendance for many people is just such a display, a "show" of faith, a hope that such evidence will convince others to join them.

Her letter went on: "Love of God and love of neighbor are inseparable." True, I thought. But there came a time for me when the balance fell off. I wanted to use the time I had left seeking Him out intimately, and loving my neighbor at a distance. Barbara wrote: "Because God's purpose is self-giving, we fulfill our purpose 'to love God and enjoy him forever' (as the Westminster Catechism puts it) by participating in God's way of being in the world, which is with and for others." True again, I suppose. But when I grew discouraged by my search for God in the world, repeating all the customary usages and practices of that search in church, I needed to try to find and know God as a Presence within. She went on to say that "private faith in God seems to me a contradiction, because God, who is perfectly sufficient without us, chose for love of us (first the people of Israel, then each of us and all of us) to be with us."

God with us, it seemed to me at this late age, is a matter of both public and private prayer. I had tried the former; I knew I was now in search of Him through the latter. That "faith is unavoidably social because God is fundamentally social," she wrote, cannot be true for everyone. Like Simone Weil, I fear the church as a social structure. Still, until three years ago, I made my way regularly into a church to participate in the liturgy, to affirm dogma aloud in the Credo and to pray, in unison most of the time, and silently, when time was allowed for it.

OUTSIDE IN

My recognition of what I was not doing in church came gradually—and late. I was not praying, but reciting, not using the well-worn words as vehicles to try to reach God, but giving easy, automatic responses, elocuting with others around me. I knew the liturgy by heart; it had worn a groove in me that cut away thought, as if the sentences were moving from my memory to my mouth without stopping for meaning in my mind.

William James, in *The Varieties of Religious Experience,* observed that in some, "religion exists as a dull habit, in others as an acute fever." To my dismay I had lost the acute fever in routine and ritual, in repetition, during the staple diet of prayer, and by what the eminent critic George Steiner in another context calls "eloquent vacuity." Perhaps I should have expected this to happen, after the long, worn usage of time. Edward Yarnold wrote about liturgy in *The Study of Spirituality:* "No one's spirituality is entirely individual. . . . [It is] shaped by public worship." I had allowed my inner life to be shaped almost entirely by the forms provided in communal worship. I had become a victim of habit and routine. My hard-won belief seemed to be barely alive when we came together.

Worse, due to my advancing age and crotchety disposition, I found myself unduly distracted by the programmed motion during the service. The stirrings of the congregation, the riffling of pages and booklets and hymnals, the sounds of kneeling, standing, and sitting, the perambulations of the assistants and the celebrants on the altar and the offering-collectors up and down the aisles, the progress of well-intentioned but unskilled lectors to and from the podium, the ushered parade to the altar to receive communion—I had not been able to find a way to blot out the constant bustle. True, it was all in obedience to official rules of conduct, but for me it left no place to pray in silence, or listen, or wait for a sense of God. "Be still, then, and know that I am God" is the familiar injunction in Psalm 46:11, but in church there was no stillness, no time in which to know Him.

A minor matter: most disturbing to me were the built-in interruptions to the liturgy itself. Priests and rectors most often prefer to make all their announcements of coming events—dinners and meetings, lectures and committee gatherings, parish suppers, and much else—in the middle of the service. Having broken into the rhythm of the liturgy for these practical matters, some community-spirited pastors then inquire if anyone in the congregation has an announcement to make. Once, I recall, a full ten minutes at the center of the rite was occupied by items of social action and plans for the winter rummage sale.

I had thought that all this commerce might be carried on before the start of the service or after the final hymn. But it was explained to me, somewhat impatiently, that congregants often arrive late or leave early, and so miss important parish business. I suggested that business be relegated to the Sunday bulletin, but this was not effective, it was said. Most people do not read it.

So, the flow of prayer is usually halted in order to inform the congregation of the potluck supper next Tuesday. God, if He has been summoned in the first moments of the liturgy, is put on hold.

Others besides me have had trouble with public prayer. In Douglas V. Steere's introduction to Thomas Merton's *Contemplative Prayer* he quotes Merton's belief that "even the liturgical life may become a short-circuit of routine and regimentation that can serve as a hiding place, a fire curtain." Merton reminded me that within the Cistercian context (which emphasizes the common, cenobitic life) St. Bernard tells us to "sit alone (*sede itaque solitarius*), have nothing in common with the crowd, nothing with the multitude of the others . . . remain alone and keep yourself for Him alone out of all others."

So, when I read in the Fourth Psalm (v. 4) "Speak to your heart in silence upon your bed," I decided to try it, to abandon corporate worship for a while. First I would find out about the experience of others with private prayer and try, at the same time, to be alone during prayer, outside the circuit of routine and regimentation, to stop, for the time being, hiding behind the fire curtain.

At first, my reading of the mystics—St. John of the Cross, Julian of Norwich, Meister Eckhart, *The Cloud of Unknowing* monk—and of more contemporary writers—William James, Henri J. M. Nouwen, Evelyn Underhill, Thomas Merton, Simone Weil, Kathleen Norris, Thomas Kelly—occupied most of my time and my thinking. I remember that I asked a friend, an ordained Episcopal priest, if she had read Simone Weil. She said no, she didn't *read* about contemplative prayer, she *did* it. And Simone Weil in *Spiritual Autobiography* says that she had never read any books to account for her extraordinary spiritual experience in Assisi. "God in his mercy had prevented me from reading the mystics, so that it should be evident to me that I had not invented this absolutely unexpected contact."

Chastened, I sorted through what I had learned from the thirty or so books piled up in my study, and turned to the practice itself. I would resort to accounts of private prayer when my practice grew stale, as I was sure it would.

PSALMS

In *The Cloister Walk* Kathleen Norris (in *Dakota*, her first book, she said she came back to religion through liturgy) warned me against a solitary journey. "Good ceremony makes room for all the dimensions of human experience in the hope that, together, we will discover something that transforms us. . . . Individuals cannot create true ceremonies for themselves alone." I hoped this was not true for everyone.

I determined to abandon ritual, to try to practice a private ceremony of worship early every morning by using the Psalms as prayer, according to the Benedictine rule. This choice was determined by the realization that Morning Prayer, which I had read for twenty years, had fallen into the grooves of rote and memory. I could no longer achieve freshness, the acute fever, by the use of it.

There was another reason to begin with the Psalms. Except for a very cursory acquaintance with those wonderful poems as they were read, one by one, during the progress of the church service, I had no real knowledge of them. Indeed, I had no time to think about them, so quickly (and sometimes poorly) were they read aloud, and then passed over, with no discussion or emphasis or exegesis, no *time* spent on them.

I was in search of new material to use as a starting point for meditation and prayer; a fresh *occasion* for prayer might be more accurate. From Kathleen Norris I learned that the Benedictines sang the Psalms daily until they reached the last one, the one hundred and fiftieth, and then they started over, a continuing cycle of prayer which, it seemed, never exhausted the possibilities of those beautiful poems. She grew to love the practice as she sang in choir with the monks (she, still a Protestant, is at the same time a Benedictine oblate). I wanted to know if I could find sustenance in them if I were *not* in a community of monks. I wished to try to create a true ceremony around the Psalms, but without the aesthetic pleasure of chant: alone.

▪

I set aside the hour between six and seven in the morning for prayer. Later I discovered that the Psalmist had chosen a similar period: "In the morning, Lord, you hear my voice; / early in the morning I make my appeal and watch for you" (5:3). Contrary to Zen practice, which requires strict posture and much bodily adherence to rule, I chose a comfortable chair where I could sit without the stresses and pains I experienced when I tried to assume the lotus position, or even a part of it. I did not want to be made more conscious of my aged body's stiffness than of the interior space I wished to explore.

Before I closed my eyes, I fixed them upon the lightening expanse of the beautiful cove beyond my window, not on a wall as some Zen Sotos prefer. Positioned thus, I watched the light of morning deepen, sometimes the raising of a sail on the small boat anchored across the water, and gulls and ducks having breakfast, without this activity occupying much more than my eyes; after some practice, I watched without seeing, or at least without being aware that I was seeing.

All I knew about the Psalms was that some almost certainly contained references to events in early Israelite history. I recalled that at first scholars had assigned their composition to King David; in the Episcopal *Book of Common Prayer* they are called, collectively, the Psalms of David. But this seems no longer to be a tenable ascription. It is now thought that the whole is actually an anthology of songs/poems from a variety of sources and pens.

I read Robert Alter's essay on the literary genres contained in the Psalms. Many fell into categories that scholars have described as praises and supplications and as love poems (to God).

Alter wrote that "the usual Hebrew title for the collection is *Tehillim*, 'Praises.'" There are as well thanksgiving songs, some of which may have been used for liturgical purposes, chanted aloud (and so the Benedictine practice is well founded), sung during ceremonies in the Temple, on the whole intended for communal use.

During the first six months of my journey through Psalms I was struck by the number of times the poet/singer asks the Lord to protect him from his adversaries. I noticed this at the start of my reading, as early as the Third Psalm. "Surely you will strike my enemies across the face; / you will break the teeth of the wicked" (3:7).

I found it hard to accept a view that these supplications all reflected angry and retributive requests for the Lord to take sides against the outside world, against social evil-doers, military adversaries, and the Israelites' enemies. It was more useful for me to believe that the Psalmists were themselves divided souls, that their enemies were within, and that they were petitioning God for assistance against the parts of themselves that were inimical to spiritual health, very much in the spirit of "Have pity on me, Lord, for I am weak; heal me, Lord, for my bones are wracked. / My spirit shakes with terror; / how long, O Lord, how long?" (6:2–3).

Much later I had a small confirmation of this view when I read that Thomas Merton in *Contemplative Prayer* called these "battle Psalms"—in that they "revealed the secret movements of the heart in its struggle against the forces of darkness." The battle Psalms "were all interpreted as referring to *the inner war* with passion and with the demons" [italics are mine].

By the third round of my reading, in the second year of prayer, my attention was caught by the verses that contained what might be considered instruction, perhaps what Alter meant when he characterized them as "wisdom" Psalms. I was struck by the number of times the poet told me how and where to pray, beginning with the line (4:4) in which the Psalmist tells his listeners not to sin but to "speak to your heart in silence upon your bed." Other modern versions translate it somewhat differently: "Ponder it on your beds, and be still" (Revised Standard Version), "Speak in your hearts, and on your beds keep silence" (New Jerusalem Bible), and the least particular in its direction, "While you rest, meditate in silence" (New English Bible).

I preferred the last version of the verses of the Fourth Psalm because it did not insist I take to my bed. I saw it as a procedural instruction, not as content for meditation. I knew that the Psalmist meant for me to be alone. But what would be, for me, the *matter* for solitary contemplative prayer? Here I had the usual difficulty of anyone who moves away from the common uses of prayer— thanksgiving for prayers granted, requests for some new need or petition. I began the period of contemplation with Merton's definition: "Prayer means yearning for the simple presence of God. It is something so much more than uttering petitions for good things."

SQUARE ROOT

Let me go back a few months in order to note what I tried to do and failed at. My practice in contemplation, during the few minutes after the reading of a psalm or psalms, was to use for reflection phrases or sentences that had captivated me. I erased all visions of the old, anthropomorphic view of God which now and then crept into my view and cleared away everything except the suggestions that arose from the words themselves.

At first, the sentence or sentences I seemed to choose were instructions for my patience. Wait for Him, be patient with His absence, sit still, do not fill His absence with useless disquietude. Everywhere I found admonishments to my restlessness. "Wait patiently for the Lord" (27:18), "Be still before the Lord / and wait patiently for him" (37:7), and the wonderful *De Profundis:* "I wait for the Lord; my soul waits for him; / in his word is my hope. / My soul waits for the Lord, more than the watchman for the morning" (130:4, 5).

I developed a curious practice in my moments of waiting to which I gave the name of prayer, nondiscursive prayer. In the blackness behind my closed eyelids I projected a small square in which were enclosed the words I was contemplating. For some reason I still do not understand, the shape of a square served me better than that of a circle or a triangle, although I tried out every geometric shape I could conjure up. I then moved the words out of the square, leaving blackness enclosed in blackness.

Patience, I thought. I tried to extend the period of nothingness each time, believing that as long as I was without words there was a chance that the sense of God's presence might come to fill completely the wordless void. Blank intention was the prayer. The Psalmist of 101:2 asks of God, "Hide not your face from me." I understood this plea, for, having abandoned the childish conception I once had of God's manlike being, I have not been able easily to fill the space with anything else. It is hard to fill the Psalmist's "face" with nothing, harder even still to cling to a vision so absent of content, so blank.

Seekers after a mode of prayer will settle contentedly for the prescribed rite of the church in public worship, finding it easier, safer, and, ultimately, more satisfying because it is so familiar. But what prayer will serve solitary worshipers alone on a sea of infinite possibility—and darkness? Often the prayers they devise lead only to a feeling of inadequacy. What shall I say to God, so that He will come to fill my sense of absence with a sense of His presence? How can I avoid despair, the feeling that the God I wait for is not here, or anywhere? The Tenth Psalm says of the wicked: "They say in their heart, 'God has forgotten; he hides his face; he will never notice'" (10:11). That poignant cry at God's absence is heard again and again throughout the Psalms: "Hide not your face from me" (27:12); "Hide not your face from your servant" (69:19). Have I not yet learned that, long before one can come close to a sense of God's presence, one must suffer a long discouragement at His absence?

FRANNY AND THE PILGRIM

I remember first coming upon a singular answer to my questions in, of all places, J. D. Salinger's story *Franny and Zooey*, first published forty years ago in *The New Yorker*. The young coed Franny Glass seems to be having what in the early fifties was called a nervous breakdown, but her symptoms—no appetite, chattering teeth, dropping out of class, turning deathly pale, feeling "rocky" and fainting—turn out to be caused by her obsession with a small "religious" book her professor had mentioned, *The Way of a Pilgrim*, by a nineteenth-century anonymous Russian peasant.

During an agonizing lunch with Lane, her date for a college weekend, she tells him about the book she has been reading on the train and now carries with her in her handbag. The Pilgrim has dedicated his life to apostolic obedience to St. Paul's command to the Thessalonians (1. 12:17) to "pray without ceasing." The prayer he uses is called the Jesus Prayer, "Lord Jesus Christ have mercy on me." Repeated constantly, "something *happens* after a while, I don't know what . . . and the words get synchronized with the person's heartbeat, and then you're actually praying without ceasing," Franny tells Lane, who is totally absorbed in the frogs' legs he is eating and bored by what he thinks of as his crazy girlfriend.

Franny cannot stop:

> But the marvelous thing is, when you first start doing it, you don't even have to have faith in what you're doing. . . . All you have to have in the beginning is quantity. Then, later on, it becomes quality by itself. . . . He [the Pilgrim] says that any name of God—any name at all—has this peculiar, self-active power of its own. . . . Even in India they tell you to meditate on OM . . . and the exact result is supposed to happen.

When Lane asks "What *is* the result?" Franny says, "You get to see God. Something happens in some absolutely nonphysical part of the heart . . . and you see God, that's all." Lane tells her it can all be explained by simple psychology. Franny excuses herself for a moment, leaves the dining room, and faints. After she has been ministered to by Lane and the manager of the restaurant she is left lying on a couch. "Alone, Franny lay quite still, looking at the ceiling. Her lips began to move, forming soundless words, and they continued to move."

There the story ends. We assume that Salinger intends that Franny will repeat the Jesus Prayer into infinity after the end of the story, presumably in the hope of seeing God.

Franny is a religious naif, entirely without faith before she encounters the Pilgrim's little book. She is ignorant of the ancient
history of the prayer: sometime between the fifth and the eighth
centuries, in the Christian East, this prayer was used by the Desert Fathers. Its form varied, but most usually it was: "Lord Jesus
Christ, Son of God, have mercy on me."

For me, the interesting thing about the prayer is not its exact
terms (for by now I was using "God" in my reductive course toward nondiscursive prayer and not the intercessory "Jesus") but
"the discipline of frequent repetition" that its practice represented. A Greek bishop, Diadochus, in the second half of the fifth
century, urged that a prayer of two words—"Lord Jesus"—and
nothing else be used. Repetition must be uniform, Sergei Hackel
writes in *The Study of Spirituality*,

> so as to bring the intellect from fragmentation to unity, from a
> diversity of thoughts and images to a state of single-minded con-
> centration. While itself an invocation in words, by virtue of its
> brevity and simplicity, the prayer . . . enables us to reach beyond
> language into silence, beyond discursive thinking into intui-
> tive awareness.

In the next century the monk Dorotheus, in Gaza, advises a dying man to say the prayer as long as he could. But when he grew
too weak the monk advised: "Then let the Prayer go; just remember God and think that he is in front of you." Kallistos Ware
writes in *The Study of Spirituality* that "the actual saying of the
Prayer . . . is only a means to an end; what really matters is the unceasing remembrance of God."

St. John Climacus's famous seventh-century work, *The Lad-
der of Divine Ascent*, urged the prayer to be a matter of a few

words: "Pray in all simplicity. . . . Our aim should be *monologia*, brevity, not *polulogia*, garrulousness." In the last two centuries there has been a revival of the use of the prayer, as Franny discovered when she found the anonymous *The Way of a Pilgrim*. That book first appeared in 1884 and represented a curious nineteenth-century phenomenon, the pilgrimages of Russian peasants to Jerusalem. "At best, extended pilgrimage might be said to correspond to a perpetual inward quest for the Kingdom of God."

H I D E A N D S E E K: The Psalms Again

It was not the Jesus Prayer itself but its principles of repetition and brevity I tried to adopt. I began to devise my own mantras from reading the Psalms. It was not easy, for my stopping places seemed always to be at cries of despair, at sentences that recorded His absence: "Why do you stand so far off, O Lord / and hide yourself in time of trouble?" (10:1), "How long, O Lord? will you forget me forever?"(13:1), and, signifying God's deafness to the Psalmist's entreaties, "Incline your ear to me and hear my words" (17:6).

In these and a dismayingly large number of other places the Psalmist echoed my feelings as I prayed. I felt only the pain of God's absence, forgetfulness, and deafness, or, perhaps, His well-hidden presence. Like the Psalmist I now ascribed all these to complete desertion, more painful because once, that brief moment on the steps fifty years ago, I knew I had been aware of God's presence. But I could not make Him return. I understood Psalm 77's poignant rehearsal of loss:

I consider the days of old;
　　I remember the years long past;

Will the Lord cast me off forever?
　　will he no more show his favor?

Has his faithful love gone forever?
　　has his promise failed for all time? (77:7–9)

Twice the Psalmist speaks of the dead weight of his soul: "Why are you so full of heaviness, O my soul?" (42:6), and again, almost at once in the next Psalm (43:5). Perhaps it was my continuing, heavy despair at the aridity of my search, but I was aware that the commanding verbs of the first third of the Psalms—"wait" "seek" "hide" "be still" "watch" "thirst" (63), "reject" (44:23), "purge" (51:8), "answer" (69:15)—were instruction for my desperation, my growing belief that my solitary prayer might have no reward. I wondered, when I came to 62:1, if, for me, the order of things in "For God alone my soul in silence waits" might more accurately be "For God my soul waits alone, in silence." I never questioned His existence, from that moment half a century ago on the steps: I asked myself how long I would be able to follow the Psalmists' repeated counsel to wait and their description of the proper climate and place in which to do so: in silence and alone.

IN NOMINE

For some time (like the *reductio* of the seven-word Jesus Prayer to the one word, Jesus) I repeated one word for my prayer: God. It fit perfectly into my black square; it seemed to forestall elaboration or decoration. It appeared in the simplest font. Then it faded slowly, like the end of a love scene in an old movie.

I knew the Hebraic view that God should not be summoned by name: It was too holy to utter. In modern Jewish writings God is still represented by dashes or by the initials JHWH, the consonants of Jahweh. I asked my priest-friend Walter about this practice. Israel, he said, after the second century B.C., no longer pronounced a name for what was boundless and infinite. Such a name would be merely a human handle, "a matter of human control" upon the Uncontrollable, a limitation on the Limitless.

The Psalmist often used Name for God. "Be joyful in God, all you lands; sing the glory of his Name" (66:1), and "Sing to God, sing praises to his Name" followed by (in one translation) "Yahweh is his Name." But some versions prefer "His Name is the Lord." The emphasis is on the substitution, or perhaps the use of a synonym, of Name for God or Lord: "I will praise the Name of God in song" (69:32).

And Isaiah (50:10): "He who walks in darkness, to whom no light appears, let him trust in the name of Yahweh, let him rely upon his God."

During my moments of contemplative prayer, walking in darkness as I was, I tried every synonym. Yahweh sounded poetic but somehow foreign on my tongue. I found I allowed connotations of Lord to insinuate themselves into my thinking: the feudal sense of the word, the emphatic maleness of it. And what happened when I tried Name?—"May his Name remain for ever" (72:17). A curious blankness, almost a meaningless vacancy afflicted me for a while, after which the word God, without my summoning it, took its place. It did not reduce my sense of distance from Him—"O God, be not far from me; come quickly to help me, O my God" (71:12)—but the simple word stayed in place, secure within the black square, reassuring me that I was calling upon God properly (for me) even if He never answered. I was grateful ("I give you thanks, O God . . . calling upon your Name" [75:1]); I thought at least I had a name for Him:

God.

Sometimes I became paranoid about my difficulties with prayer, feeling that I was being followed into my solitary moments by doubts about the proper, useful word or words, doubts about using any word or words at all, doubts that legislated against my success in experiencing any trace of Him. The Psalmist complained that his enemies were hounding him. They had banded together and "lie in wait, they spy upon my footsteps" (56). "How the mighty gather together against me" (59), and "[They] seek my life to destroy it" (63:9). I too had my enemy—doubt—and the omnipresent intrusion of words for Him.

But, once again, I was consoled by the idea that the Psalmist/poet, in *his* paranoia, may have been using metaphor to confront his interior division, the evils within that were the enemy of his peace. The doubts that hounded me about the method I was trying were *my* interior enemies as I searched for God. I vowed to spend no more time on them. "The human mind and heart are a mystery," the Psalmist told me (64:7). I would accept the fact of mystery, and live within it to advance my private cause.

TERRA INCOGNITA

The self, always one's worst enemy, often wanders without guidance in the unknown territory of prayer. "Such is the way of those who foolishly trust in themselves" (49:12) brought me up short one day and turned my meditation into that sinkhole of ego, that all-absorbing self I recognized as the true barrier to prayer, myself. Worse was my reliance on the prose that comes from me, because the verse concludes: "and the end of those who delight in their own words."

One's own words: how tricky, even deceptive, they are, how lacking in authenticity, how far from exact. How foolish I was to trust them to lead me toward a sense of God. In an essay entitled "Style," Howard Nemerov remarked that Gustave Flaubert wanted to write a novel about nothing. I thought, in somewhat the same sense, I was that great novelist's companion in that desire; I wanted to reduce meditative prayer to nothing, no words, because I had begun to distrust the vehicle of words. Close to the end of the great cycle of poems the Psalmist cries out: "Set a watch before my mouth, O Lord / and guard the door of my lips" (141:3). I read that again and again, hoping to shut down the self-involved mechanisms that had produced my words so effortlessly when I was younger, and even now raced to my pen more fluently than was good for my writing.

But self: the intimate of words, most of which, in a lifetime, are devoted to that subject alone. My words—about me and mine, about *my* past behind the slowly closing doors of my memory, about the present, in desperation at my ailments, weaknesses, aging, and pain, and about a future, ridden by doubts and uncertainties—no longer serve my purpose and only distract me when I try to find one useful word for God. The Psalmist promises the Lord: "I will keep watch upon my ways, so that I do not offend with my tongue. . . . I will put a muzzle on my mouth. . . . So I held my tongue and said nothing" (39:1–3).

By chance, as I was thinking about the burden of self in prayer,

I read Penelope Fitzgerald's *The Knox Brothers*, a biography of her father and uncles. One uncle, Wilfred Knox, an extraordinary Episcopal priest (his brother was the equally extraordinary Roman Catholic priest Ronald Knox), came to the end of his life at seventy-nine with the conviction that, in his biographer-niece's words, he had failed lamentably "to live up to the ideals by which [his] life should be governed." Fitzgerald quoted his words at a final retreat:

> He wanted to say something about forgetfulness of self, not as a means of salvation . . . but as something necessary for its own sake. "We think of ourselves as so many billiard balls, moving up and down an infinite table, charged with the duty of avoiding collision as far as possible." But avoidance of collision is not enough, compassion is not enough, even sharing is not enough. We need to think of ourselves as nothing. "After all, it should not be so difficult."

Wilfred Knox "recalled a remark of St. Francis de Sales, that if our self-love dies half an hour before we do, we shall have done well."

St. Augustine: *Novarium te, novarium me.* "May I know you, may I know myself." I thought about those words; I wondered if it would be better for me to pray, "May I know you, may I forget myself."

During the process of trying to empty my box of my words, dislocating them from the strong pull toward my self, I tried to concentrate on the space between words, attempting to widen that neutral territory, the no-word's land of emptiness. Often, those spaces seemed to grow. At times I found I could dispense with words, even the One Word, entirely. But how nearly impossible it is, for any length of time, for someone who has spent her life relying upon words to fill her time and life to rid her prayer of them. And how equally difficult it is to try, as Wilfred Knox did, at the end of one's own life, to shake off *amour propre.* The self, which some call the soul, clings leechlike to the core of one's being, reminding one constantly of its presence, making pure prayer hard.

Simone Weil (quoted in the introduction to *The Simon Weil Reader*) knew this: "We possess nothing in this world other than the power to say I. This is what we should yield up to God."

I became aware that all too frequently I felt I was nothing but self. I could not move out or over or beyond it. I was its prisoner, absorbed in it, so I could not rid myself of that terrible warden over everything I tried to do, especially to pray.

THE BLANK OF PAIN

Wilfred Knox wrote that in extreme illness the soul "fetches its prayer" as the body fetches its breath. A year after my entry into the dark places of contemplative prayer I was given the occasion to try out this thesis.

With no warning, on a trip to Washington, D.C., I was afflicted with a disease called shingles, more elaborately, varicella–herpes zoster. This, I was to learn, is the same virus that causes chicken pox. When that childhood disease is over, its virus takes up permanent residence in the spinal nerves where it hides out until something, usually in the aging person, activates it. It enters the peripheral sensory nerve receptors and came upon me rather benignly with outward manifestations of blisters. Within a few hours I took medication. In seven days, the ugly, wormlike blisters broke and disappeared. That should have been the end of the invasion, but no, the virus took possession of one side of the middle section of my body. It acquired a new, less-down-to-earth name, post-herpetic neuralgia, wiping away the more common, building-supplies connotation of shingles.

Medical literature describes the pain as "excessive," "acute," "severe," "relentless." None of these describe adequately the searing effect of a cramped hand clutched tightly to the side, front, and back, from spine to mid-rib, and never for a moment loosening its grip. At first I believed that something—drugs, the nutritional therapy of herbs, homeopathic treatment, heat, cold, nakedness (the least touch of clothing and bedding was excruciating), and, finally, morphine patches—would alleviate what one handbook reduced to the relatively gentle word "distress." An acupuncturist my friend Sybil consulted did not encourage me to try his treatment.

A tangent: I was recommended to another physician described as a specialist in "pain management." His office was some distance from my house, but nonetheless I drove there to consult him, so desperate was I for relief. He said the only effective procedure was a sympathetic block, during which a shunt of sorts is inserted into the nerve roots and then injected every day for a week with analgesics and other substances that I cannot now remember. He added the warning that it would have to be done within the next several weeks or it would have no effect. At this point I was unfortunately reminded of the new-car salesman insisting I buy his car today because of its very limited discount.

I shuddered at the prospect of a fifty-mile drive every day for a week and, worse, the idea of the implant in my back. I asked the pain expert if he had done many of these procedures. "Oh yes," he replied. I wanted to know the name of some recipients of the treatment so I could inquire of them about it. He said there were none up here in Maine "because local primary care physicians are not sympathetic to the idea."

"On whom, then, *did* you do it?"

"On tourists."

Of course, he may have been right; it might have helped the pain. But as a "local" I was turned away by the humor of his words. Then, after two weeks of resorting to morphine patches during which time I seemed to lose control of my consciousness and to enter a realm of near-madness, I gave up on finding anything to alleviate the pain. I had to accept the continuing fact of it: "There is no known, consistently reliable, preventive therapy or definitive treatment for permanent relief of established postherpetic neuralgia," one textbook concluded.

To turn the intractable pain to some positive use, I decided to try to live with full awareness of its presence. Always before, while I prayed, I tried to ignore it. Now I thought I might try to include it, to use it as a presence. Dostoevsky's Sonya in *Crime and Punishment* urges her murderer/lover to "accept suffering and redeem yourself by it"; and the policeman Porfiry tells Raskolnikov the story of Mikolka who wanted to "embrace suffering." I have always found it hard to believe this "embrace" of Mikolka's. I questioned it even more after six months of post-herpetic neuralgia pain. But I could believe in acceptance.

Many times I wondered, Should I pray for the lifting of the pain during my period of contemplation? This seemed somehow unworthy. Bad and constant as it was, I knew many others who had to bear far worse. If I were to change my first aim of prayer—to wait for a sense of His presence—I could ask for relief, but I was committed to waiting. I could not pray to alleviate the horren-

dous state of my body. Unlike Sonya, I had never considered re-
demption as the end of prayer, but I thought perhaps I could accept suffering as an element of it.

It did not work. Prayer was not acceptance; it was the mortal
victim of pain. In a poem by Emily Dickinson, #650 in *The Complete Poems*, I found a definition, and prognosis, for my affliction:

> Pain—has an element of Blank—
> It cannot recollect
> When it begun—or if there were
> A time when it was not—
>
> It has no Future—but itself—
> Its Infinite contain
> Its Past—enlightened to perceive
> New Periods—of Pain.

At this time, by luck, I came upon another work by Simone
Weil. In *Letter to Joe Bousquet*, written a year before her death,
she tells her correspondent of an affliction that sounded very
much like mine:

But my attitude toward myself . . . a mixture of contempt and
hatred and repulsion, is to be explained on a lower level—the
level of biological mechanisms. For twelve years I have suffered
from pain around the central point of the nervous system. . . .
This pain persists during sleep and has never stopped for a second. For a period of ten years it was so great, and was accompanied by such exhaustion, that the effort of attention and intellectual work was usually [as] despairing. . . . My efforts seemed
completely sterile and without any temporary result.

I spent several weeks of anguished uncertainty whether death was not my imperative duty. . . . I was only able to calm myself by deciding to live conditionally, for a trial period.

In another place Weil writes: "Affliction makes God appear to be absent for a time, more absent than a dead man, more absent than light in the utter darkness of a cell." Like Job, one must go on loving God in the emptiness or at least go on wanting to love. If one stops, "God's absence becomes final."

My time of intense pain, my constant companion, was a useful period because I learned that emptiness, as Weil terms it, or "Blank" in Dickinson's word, caused by omnipresent pain stopped me dead (not my favorite figure of speech), made prayer of any kind impossible. Later, in a strange way, pain permitted me to stand apart from prayer, not to pray but to think about prayer as a *Ding an sich.* I considered what I might try once my self-absorption was conquered. I thought of prayer as an intellectual exercise, a blueprint for future practice, but not the practice itself; theory, nothing more.

PRAYER

> Nothing is more difficult than prayer. In all other tasks of religious life, however exacting, one can sometimes rest, but there is no rest in prayer, up to the end of one's life.
>
> —Simone Weil, Introduction to
> *The Simone Weil Reader*

I had already learned that "prayer is far more than the passive reception of the Church's liturgical life," as Sergei Hackel paraphrases the thought of the Russian priest John of Kronstadt in

The Study of Spirituality. I began to discover other things in my prayerless period of exploration. "Prayer needs to be daring, sincere, attentive, unrelenting, inward" was John's definition. Yet, "inward" did not rule out for him liturgical, especially eucharistic, prayer. In fact, he wrote, in *My Life in Christ,* that the experience of blessedness and spiritual tranquillity that comes in church "is a foretaste of that infinite bliss those of us who see God's face will experience eternally."

"Inward" applied to prayer. Where, under what circumstances, I wondered once again. Might inward prayer be achieved in church, as John thought? Why had it not been possible for me? I remembered the persons I had watched in church who seemed so completely absorbed in the liturgy, unaware, it appeared, and unaffected by its routine and rote. For them, and for the others making less stringent demands upon prayer, those for whom prayer consists mainly in reciting publicly the usual petitions (often in unison) for the church, for safety, health, protection, relief from suffering and acceptance of death, for oneself and for others, church must be there to serve their purposes.

In my months of pain when I could not pray and spent my time searching the literature of prayer, I found four most valuable guides. From them, Simone Weil, Thomas Merton, Thomas Kelly, *The Cloud of Unknowing,* and from some others, I learned what I needed to know—and go on needing to know still.

THOMAS MERTON

Twice during his tragically short life (he died in Bangkok by accident at the age of fifty-three) the poet/monk Thomas Merton wrote what were intended to be a monk's instructions to his fellow Trappists for the way to live an interior life. He wished to plant the seeds for successful contemplative prayer. This intention might have ruled me out of his audience had not Merton, in his introduction to his last book, *Contemplative Prayer*, included me in his remarks. "Every Christian [for which I wish he had written "everyone" since such prayer is surely of concern to persons of every faith] ought, theoretically at least, to have enough interest in prayer to be able to read and make use of what is here said for monks, adapting it to the circumstances of their own vocation." But what he wrote, he said, was applicable to anyone with faith, "though perhaps with a little less emphasis on the intensity of certain trials which are proper to the life of solitude."

The first book of Merton's I read, in 1949, *Seeds of Contemplation*, seemed to have passed through my hands and eyes without ever affecting my thinking or my actions. I read it two years after those moments on the steps. Had I taken notice of a few of Merton's words I would have perhaps not followed the well-worn path of more than fifty years through the liturgies of churches.

Perhaps I would have noted his warning that my Millwood moments were very dangerous, because I, like the monks to whom he was addressing his book, did not understand "these experiences, these manifestations and curiosities, which may or may not be supernatural." His words for them are belittling: "outbursts," "feelings of intoxication," "excitements," and, most disturbing of all, "staggering intoxication of the senses." Had I taken him at his word I would have made a greater effort to put my "curiosity," as he called it, behind me.

Later in the book he returned to cautions against deceptive "emotional religious ferment," "sensible intoxication," "movements of passions," "excitements," "moments of spiritual joy," and, worst of all, "this staggering drunkenness of the senses," all of which I took personally, as they say, as criticisms of my Mill-wood experience: it had all been deceptive, blinding, self-absorbed, and so to be violently resisted. My faith in what I had experienced was severely shaken. Had I been deluding myself? Had my memory exaggerated those moments? How wrong-headed my lifelong attempts had been to recover them.

In contrast to his account of a false, self-deluded religious experience, there was young Merton's description of what contemplation truly consists in: "a sudden emptying of the soul in which images vanish and concepts and words are silent"; the arrival at "a desert of aridity"; a place of darkness, dryness, and "arid quietude"; and finally, the achievement of tranquillity—"a luminous and absorbing experience of love . . . from the depth of this cloud . . . the voice of God speaking without words."

Oh *then*, apparently, it may have been what happened to me, the "tides of joy that are concentrated into strong touches . . . a flash of flame that blazes in the soul . . . and sometimes burns with a wound that is delectable although it gives pain." But how was I to distinguish between what I remembered I had felt and what Merton saw as false self-delusion? Was not mine a true luminous experience? Had I been in a deep cloud of mistaken elation, or, as I believed, had I been surrounded by something I called the sense of Presence?

STRONG TOUCHES

Now I took up *Seeds of Contemplation* again. I noticed with interest that Merton had written the book in the Abbey at Gethsemani while he was quite young, not yet ordained a priest and, if one noticed the number of lyrical paradoxes, still very much a poet. Try as I might I could not move past such puzzling formulations as "We become contemplatives when God discovers Himself in us," and "God utters me like a word containing a thought of Himself." I did not know what they meant, but I began to suspect they were more poetic than wise.

I was disturbed by how often the poet/monk spoke for God, or told me what was in His mind: "It is true that God knows Himself in all things that exist," and "Contemplation has been planned for us by God as our true and proper element." How could Merton know? How could he presume to know? How many times, in other books that offered to guide me in the proper way to pray, have I come upon the same kind of omniscient sentence. They always begin: "God knows . . ." and "God thinks . . ."

Contradictions abound in Merton's thought. "The ultimate perfection of the contemplative life" requires that we see God in men. "The more we are alone with God the more we are united with one another," and "The silence of contemplation is deep and rich and endless society, not only with God but with men." But then, further into the book he describes interior solitude as "an abyss opening up in the center of your own soul"; and "it is in the deepest darkness that we most fully possess God on earth." He suggests that one must withdraw from all exterior things, from "thoughts and concerns of temporal existence," in order to meditate properly, "to become aware of the presence of God."

I was struck by the young monk's certainty that "all experience of God comes to us through Christ." I found this a stumbling block, for I had just arrived, in my own idiosyncratic journey, at a crisis of thought in which Jesus no longer seemed to me to be an inevitable intercessory. Could it be because much of my prayer life depended on the Psalms? Was it because, by not attending church, by waiting alone for the sense of God, the presence of His mortal Son no longer seemed necessary to my search?

Only once, in one sentence in the book, does Merton refer to public worship, and then it seems an offhand acknowledgment, a secondary, almost throw-away consolatory thought: "Above all [after learning how to meditate everywhere, "waiting for a bus or riding in a train"] enter into the Church's liturgy and make the liturgical cycle part of your life—let its rhythm work its way into your body and soul."

There were other, very good and useful (to me) things here. I felt at one with Merton when he asks, "What good does it do to say a few formal prayers to Him and then turn away and give all my mind and all my will to created things?" I had come to this question too. It was not only that I had rebelled against prescribed rite, habit, and routine, but that I knew how easy it was for me to go down the steps of the church, leaving all thought of God behind, under the comfortable but mistaken notion that I had prayed enough; now I could return to worldly living, to "created things." I remember how, as a Roman Catholic, I was told to be sure to "do my Easter duty." Duty was the operative word; coming out of church on Easter Sunday in all the years that followed was I not filled with self-satisfaction, that worst of all sins, that I had done my duty?

Merton's words about detachment interested me. At first he

warned monks not to become attached to pious practice, not to meditation or a special system of spirituality, tendencies I found I too had to guard against. For a long time I had been attached to one rite, one set of prescribed pious practices. And then, as I moved away from them, I formed new attachments to my own place and way of praying, only to find my attention to my self blinding and deafening to the Sense I was seeking. "The secret of interior peace is detachment," writes Merton, continuing, in his love of paradox: "You will never be able to have perfect interior peace and recollection until you are detached even from the desire for peace and recollection. You will never be able to pray perfectly until you are detached from the pleasure of prayer."

First, to achieve detachment: how difficult, how much will and determination it takes; and then to become detached from the pleasure of achieving it, how far must I go beyond the first difficulty? While I was thinking about this I happened to reread Simone Weil's essay, *Concerning the Our Father* and came upon another paradox: "We must cast aside all other desires [among them, the hope of the coming of the Kingdom of God] for the sake of our desire for eternal life, but we should desire eternal life itself with renunciation." And then her terrifying conclusion, expressed in her usual extremist way: *"We must not even become attached to detachment."* These are my italics, representing astonishment at how hard this would be, how far I had to go to achieve it, and then what? I was overwhelmed by the question, To be detached from detachment—is this a clever paradox, or a truly achievable state of being?

Seeds of Contemplation contained other warnings to me. I cannot leave the world and hide myself in solitude because I will take the world (an unquiet city where people fight to possess things) with me into solitude. If I flee the selfish world I will find myself alone with my own selfishness, which will give the devil possession of me or drive me mad. So, "it is dangerous to go into solitude merely because *you happen to like to be alone.*"

The exclamatory italics are mine. How close to the bone this cut. But then I was mollified by Merton's quick adjoinder that physical solitude, exterior silence, "are all morally necessary for anyone who wants to lead a contemplative life." I was brought up short again by what followed: "We look for solitude in order to grow there in love for God and in love for other men." This zigzagging of thought, between the world of persons and my solitary world, dizzied me. But surely such warning must be necessary. I began to wonder if a long practice of private prayer would inevitably bring me back to "men," as Merton in his unreconstructed nomenclature termed them, and public prayer.

At the last, I was grateful for this early work of Merton's which contained a fine prayer. In these days of trying to look at prayer as a means to an End, I used it often when I tried to write for publication. He asks God,

Keep me from loving money in which is hatred, from avarice and ambition that suffocate my life. Keep me from the vain works of vanity and the thankless labor in which artists destroy themselves for pride and money and reputation.

I chose among Merton's many suggestions, following his direction to "use what helps you and avoid what gets in your way." I was determined to make this my motto, for all choices and considerations, for all the words I used, and those I put away from me.

Searching for modes of prayer and content, at first I would settle for the wish to find them. Merton said: "The will to pray is the essence of prayer, and the desire to find God."

Still, I thought, there was an inordinate amount of self in my search for what might help me, for what I could use and not use, for what to do and not to try to do. Merton, and others I was reading, warned me not to rely upon myself for very much, except perhaps for the use of will. "The most dangerous man in the world is the contemplative who is guided by nobody."

DEAR WALTER

I have been reading books by persons who seem to me to have known a great deal about interior prayer, mainly Simone Weil and Thomas Merton. I am impressed by Weil's need for a guide, Father Jean-Marie Perrin, to whom she wrote letters of inquiry and, at last, a confession of her spiritual agonies and hard-won iconoclastic beliefs.

Merton, writing from his monastery, advised his fellow monks that spirits truly drawn to God through contemplative prayer will overcome their own selfishness and blindness of judgment by seeking the guidance of another. This brought me to thinking of you often, after our long lunches, and then before I settled down to prayer, and later, reading about prayer. You have become a guide Thomas Merton urged me to seek. But I too seldom do, so engaged am I in the struggle to escape from self.

I have been interested in the book you lent me, *The Study of Spirituality*, especially the early chapter by Edward Yarnold in which he speaks of "media of spirituality," by which I think he means liturgies. He begins with an especially disturbing (to me) paragraph: "No one's spirituality is entirely individual. Spirituality is shaped by public worship; and conversely forms and styles of public worship are conditioned by the spirituality of the worshipping community."

If the first part of his statement is true, I have been going against the direction he describes, seeking a way of private prayer after turning away from unsatisfying (to me) liturgy, rather than a mode of prayer that has been shaped by it. And what is perhaps worse, I have not seen in "forms and styles of public worship" very much evidence of the presence of individual spirituality.

This worries me. Tell me, am I so caught in a web of self and self-imposed mode of worship that my practices drive me into deadly dormancy? Here I started to use the word "quietude" and at once remembered reading in the same book a chapter on Fénelon and Quietism which pushed me further into asking myself, How far have I gone into this now discredited seventeenth-century belief?

From Elfrieda Dubois's brief summary in *The Study of Spirituality* I learned about the colorful life of Madame Guyon who with a Barnabite-priest friend Father La Combe studied the methods of spiritual prayer and then traveled about with him to teach their doctrine, the use of mental prayer to achieve "complete abandonment into the hands of God." Inevitably I suppose, their partnership and "mutual exaltation" was often taken to be immoral behavior. As punishment, Father La Combe was sent to prison where he went mad and died. Madame Guyon was confined in a convent.

Upon her release she was introduced to Archbishop Fénelon.

She thought "their minds sympathized"; she found in him "another self," as she wrote to a friend. What they agreed on was complete detachment from sense images in prayer in order to allow for a feeling of the pure presence of God. For them, achieving this sense had nothing whatever to do with the abandonment of sin and so allowed for a complete disregard for morality. Opponents saw the practice as contrary to following one's Christian duty and moral dictates.

Archbishop Fénelon disagreed with Madame Guyon's view that after the soul makes this total abandonment to God through prayers of quietude, no further effort of any kind is required. But he continued to believe in the use of passive mental prayer and cited as his authorities all the great mystics and theologians, including St. Augustine, St. John of the Cross, and St. Francis de Sales (who wrote that God's will was expressed in the soul when it is in a state of indifference). The Bishop of Meaux, to whom the Archbishop had recommended Madame Guyon, found her to be a false prophetess and descried her "dangerous spiritual effusions" (did this not sound like Merton's verbiage?).

So the dispute about what was then termed Quietism grew to enormous proportions. The controversy was referred to the King, Louis XIV, and then sent to Rome. Fénelon was condemned, but agreed to abandon his belief that when the self is entirely excluded from one's consciousness, absolute indifference is achieved. In a passive state of contemplation, one is able to reach the pure love of God. He was completely reconciled with the church and died just before he was to be made a cardinal.

I have no idea what became of Madame Guyon. Fénelon's views continued to have followers in the next centuries. I find myself one of them, because he spoke so often of ways to approach *the pure love of God,* a concept I had wrongly taken for granted, as a given, and of the total abandonment of self-interest. Dubois sums up his thought: "The notion of indifference, that is love indifferent to any self-interest, but only complying with the will of God, belongs to a state of passivity. . . . For Fénelon indifference means to be free from all satisfaction, even the most subtle spiritual one." No doubt you know all this already. I rehearse it for myself rather than for you. Do you see any danger in thinking this way? Are there hidden pitfalls? Am I indeed a Quietist?

P.S. I have also been looking into the sixteenth-century beliefs of Huldreich Zwingli (quoted by C. M. Dent in *The Study of Spirituality*): "Before I say anything or listen to the teaching of man, I will first consult the mind of the Spirit of God. . . . And then go on to the Gospels. . . . You must be *theodidacti,* that is, taught of God, not man." Prayer, he believed, should be simple, without music or choir, and require no intermediaries such as saints or the Virgin (but he did allow for Jesus). It is disturbing, is it not, that the more I read, the more I seem to come upon views that underline mine. Am I ignoring the others, passing over them? Please inform.

JULIAN THE ANCHORESS

My pain increased, then stuck fast at its immoderate level, and never diminished for a moment. In the months of affliction my ability to pray was lost. When I found in her *Revelations of Divine Love* Julian of Norwich's definition of prayer—the deliberate, persevering action of the soul—I tried to apply the force of her adjectives, deliberate, persevering, to my weakened will. While they kept me at it for a few moments, the pain always managed to intervene and then defeat me. It was not that I did not wish to pray or that I could not reenter the black square of my concentration, but that I felt deeper despair than ever before at the emptiness I found there, the silence, God's unavailability. "So He says . . . Pray inwardly," Julian wrote, "even if you do not enjoy it. . . . For when you are dry, empty, sick or weak, at such time is your prayer most pleasing to me."

Dame Julian of Norwich was not putting words ("God says . . .") into the Lord's mouth; she heard Him speak to her during her "shewings." In May 1373 when she was thirty years old she suffered an almost fatal illness. During that time she received sixteen revelations, or showings, or appearances of the Lord to her, in a very short time—fifteen in a single day, and the last in the day following. She wrote an account of them soon after they occurred. Then, twenty years later, after she had lived in seclusion, she wrote a longer version, the result of her long meditation upon what had appeared to her.

Modern readers of her book concentrate on her startling (for her time) account of "the motherhood of God" as revealed to her by the Lord. She speaks of "our Mother Christ" and says: "This fine and lovely word *Mother* . . . cannot be properly used of any but him." God is "our Mother in nature and grace." In the creation of us, God had been both kindly Father and "God all-wise our kindly Mother." Mother Julian may have been the first feminist mystic; it is cheering to find that early spiritual thought was once couched in these contemporary terms. Later patristic formulations did not allow for anything but male designations: God the Father, God the Son, Lord.

Convinced feminist that I am, it was not this aspect of Julian's life and work that interested me most, but the account of her direct experiences with God. There seems to be very little doubt about the reality of her sickness, according to Clifton Waltors who translated Julian's Middle English; modern scholars view it as "not hysterical in origin." As to the revelations, they are accepted as genuine or not, I suppose, according to the reader's inclination. Scholars do agree, however, that "the evidence supports the view that this rather down-to-earth and practical woman [she was not yet an anchoress when the Lord, as she wrote, showed Himself to her, but living at home and apparently cared for in her illness by her mother] received insight into matters about which it is unlikely she could have had informed and balanced views."

Julian calls herself "unlettered," but no doubt her re-visioned account (which we now read) may have been accompanied by embellishment, as Wolters points out. Still, I considered her a valuable addition to my short list of persons—headed by Simone Weil—who, in one way or another, had an experience distantly related to mine. Dame Julian's were manifold and rich, full of bloody and beautiful symbols and stories the Lord seems to have shown and told her. But because of my moment on the steps, I could accept the reality of her report: "And the bodily sight stinted, but the spiritual sight dwelled in my understanding and I abode with reverent dread joying in what I saw."

Sometimes I wondered at the literal reality of what Julian said she had seen. Might not it have been a literary embodiment of wishful thinking? For did not Moses Maimonides, in *Guide for the Perplexed*, warn that "man should only believe what he can grasp with his intellectual faculties, or perceive by his senses, or what he can accept on trustworthy authority." Was Dame Julian trustworthy? Could I "joy" in what I had seen? I wanted very much to think so.

MERTON AGAIN

Someone had given me Merton's book on Zen. In it I found much of value. But as you might by now expect I centered on his discussion of Buddhism, Christianity, and pain. He noted that both faiths regard ordinary human existence as "material for a radical transformation of consciousness." Since life is full of confusion and suffering, he went on, one should make good use of them "to transform one's confusion and suffering."

This came close to the old Catholic practice I was once taught, to "offer up" as penance whatever was displeasing or painful, indeed, suffering of every sort. Making use of suffering by applying it to something outside of myself, outside of the pain that is, is this what he meant? Could I do this? Was I like the man who tries to explain suffering "in order to evade it"? No, I had it wrong. Merton thought that suffering was not a problem, something we could solve and therefore escape. "[It] is part of our very ego-identity and empirical existence." Enter into it, and hope to be transformed by it.

To my selective and idiosyncratic way of believing, the culminating event of the life of Jesus was not the Resurrection but the Crucifixion. We who are in pain hardly to be compared to his could empathize with his anguished cry of desertion which he echoed from the Psalms (22:1): "My God, my God, why have you forsaken me?" This was his humanity speaking. The unresponsive silence of God that followed was what I was experiencing when the ability to pray left me.

If I knew anything in this worst of times it was "the wisdom of emptiness," a phrase provided me by Merton when he reported his conversations with the Zen philosopher Daietz Suzuki. The Psalmist's query to God: "Why do you stand so far off, O Lord / and hide yourself in time of trouble?" (10:1), and the admission: "Darkness is my only companion" (88:19), and the plea: "O God, do not keep silent" (83:1)—these I found myself echoing. I could not find a way to use pain to associate my state with Jesus on the Cross; I could only reflect weakly his despair at having been abandoned, left in the dark, in the silence of rejection (I thought), in the terrible game of hide-and-seek God seemed to be playing with me: "How long will you hide yourself, O Lord?" (89:46).

COMMUNITY OF ONE

An anxious, solitary practitioner of contemplative prayer, I found myself at times thinking of the abandoned pleasures of prayer in community. I was reminded of this by reading Dietrich Bonhoeffer's *Life Together*, a disturbing book that challenged my thought. Most of the book concerned the blessings of living in "visible fellowship" with fellow Christians. To him, "the physical presence of other Christians is a source of incomparable joy and strength to the believer."

He writes that only through the Word of God in Jesus Christ, which is never achieved ("spoken to him") privately ("In himself he is destitute and dead"), can we approach salvation and righteousness. From the outside will the Word come.

There was worse for me. I was the "visionary dreamer" whom, Bonhoeffer was sure, "God hates." How he knows this I cannot imagine. But since God (again we enter the fanciful realm of God's known views) has bound us together in one body with other Christians, we should come together early in the morning to praise Him: "Morning," he was sure, "does not belong to the individual, it belongs to the Church of the triune God, to the Christian family, to the brotherhood." He has decided, "Common life under the Word begins with common worship at the beginning of the day." I was disturbed as I read on, especially when Bonhoeffer assured me that my beloved Psalms were not mine to pray alone. They belong

> not to the individual member but to the whole Body of Christ. Only in the whole Christ does the whole Psalter become a reality, a whole in which the individual can never fully comprehend and call his own. This is why the prayer of the psalms belongs in a peculiar way to the fellowship.

Pastor Bonhoeffer understands Psalm 5 as an instruction in the way to pray. He asks, "Is this not a hint that one who prays never prays alone?" His question sent me back to Psalm 5, which begins with what might be taken to be a temporal placement of prayer in solitude: "Give ear to my words, O Lord; consider my meditation. . . . In the morning, Lord, you hear my voice; early in the morning I make my appeal and watch for you." But to Bonhoeffer, the true determination of where one prays comes in verse 7. "But as for me, through the greatness of your mercy I will go into your house; I will bow down toward your whole temple in awe of you."

Perhaps because of his role as pastor Bonhoeffer is sure that all worship should be public, that the only way to God is through fellowship and community. For most of his book he explores methods of accomplishing these ends in the family and in the congregation. At the last, almost as an afterthought, he devotes several pages to directions and warnings about the part of the day one might spend alone.

Here, Bonhoeffer's admonitions are twofold: if I am afraid of being alone I should not seek community, he says, and, reversely, "Let him who is not in community beware of being alone." Like Merton he is fond of paradox: "Only as we are within the fellowship can we be alone, and only he that is alone can live in the fellowship." Even periods of silence and solitude have their dangers: "One who seeks solitude without fellowship perishes in the abyss of vanity, self-infatuation and despair."

Is this what has happened to me? Certainly it is a warning that I need to be aware of. For, perhaps wrongly, I have sought solitude in absence *from* fellowship. I am therefore, as many writers on spiritual matters have thought, in danger of assault by all the worldly devils; I am vulnerable to the sins Bonhoeffer has enumerated. Self is my enemy, especially the self alone.

What of meditation? In Bonhoeffer's view the time devoted to this act should be strictly defined. Meditation should be "devoted to the Scriptures, private prayer, and intercession, *and it has no other purpose*" [italics are mine]. I am not to spend my time in "spiritual experiments." I am to confine my meditative time to the reading of a brief, selected text from Scripture and ponder this text to find what it is saying to me personally. It is a cerebral activity; it is not necessary that "we should have any unexpected, extraordinary experience in meditation." And, he warns, if I do have such an experience it is a mistake to take it seriously.

Prayer, he wrote, springs out of the reading of Scripture. Following that, I must make my intercessions in an orderly, somewhat dogmatic fashion. I am given a list of proper intercessions for those things that are appropriate to ask for privately: "the clarification of our day, for preservation from sin, for growth in sanctification, for faithfulness and strength in our work"; and for those I have had no time to pray for in corporate prayer.

Bonhoeffer saw religion as a practice of the "fellowship" and its leader. If he acknowledged that "often a ritual becomes an evasion of real prayer," a small nod to my difficulty, he was more concerned that any desire for special prayer fellowships, "any individual undertakings of this kind may well plant the seed of destruction in the community."

I thought I recognized in Bonhoeffer's thought the firm hand of a minister whose profession is public, whose sphere is the congregation, and for whom theology is a subject to be strictly taught. In his professional view, the parishioner who leaves the pew to try another path is liable to every kind of spiritual danger. I was shaken by the realization that, because of his reputation for wisdom, he might be entirely right and I in my ignorance entirely wrong.

Bonhoeffer speaks of the *table fellowship* of Christians, the celebration of the Eucharist performed in church, at the altar. For me, this was the last station of my church climb, the final stop at which I hoped to feel some sense of God's presence. During the two years of my absence from this culminating act of Christian public worship I missed it, although I could not be sure what I missed, the hope, the possibility that God might be present there, or the significance of the symbols.

But to Bonhoeffer, one's presence at the table [his word for altar], the reception with others of the *one* bread that is given and received, meant that we are linked together in fellowship "in a firm covenant." The sacrament is a sign, larger than itself, that is meaningful if it is received during public prayer in company: "The life of Christians together under the Word has reached its perfection in the sacrament."

I was worried that not receiving the sacrament put me outside the Church. I wanted very much to believe, as Simone Weil did, that there was room for the churchless in the body of the Church. "I do not believe that I am outside the Church as far as it is a source of sacramental life; only so far as it is a social body," she wrote to her friend Father Perrin a year before she died.

On the last page of *Life Together* I saw that my solitary study of its contents was not what was envisioned by the publisher. Suggested to me for purchase is a leader's guide to "a discussion group with step-by-step instructions, questions, journaling exercises and group activities for a six-session program."

It was entirely suitable that a book celebrating the virtues of fellowship in life and prayer should be urged by the publisher upon groups for discussion of its meaning. Group thought, group practice, group activities (what in the world could *these* be?) are the preferred methods of modern study, gatherings useful in the pursuit of some kinds of knowledge in seminars, classes, and workshops. But the mind is not a group instrument. It does better left to its own devices, going its way in single file. For me, only alone, in the silence of my room, am I able to achieve any sort of genuine understanding or insight.

Simone Weil feared that in group discussions "collective language begins to dominate," and in *Waiting for God* she cites Christ's words about his presence among us: "He said precisely that he always forms the third in the intimacy of the tête-à-tête." But suppose one waits for God alone?

HERBERT AND GOD

For a few days I was preoccupied with Bonhoeffer's insistence upon fellowship in every aspect of life and his implied devaluation of meditation and contemplative prayer. I thought about it around the edges of my own prayer which by now had become almost wordless. I remembered Simone Weil's account in *Spiritual Autobiography* of her meeting in Solesmes with a young English Catholic soon after her visit to Assisi. He told her about the metaphysical English poets of the seventeenth century, and she discovered a particular poem by George Herbert that she was taken with. She memorized it and said it over and over until it took on what she called the virtue of a prayer. Then, startlingly, "It" happened to her again. "It was during one of these recitations that . . . Christ himself came down and took possession of me." She calls the encounter "a real contact, person to person, here below, between a human being and God." She felt, she said, "the presence of a love."

Herbert's poem is called "Love"—his synonym for "God" or "Lord":

> Love bade me welcome; yet my soul drew back,
>   Guilty of dust and sin.

But quick-eyed Love, observing me grow slack
    From my first entrance in,
Drew nearer to me, sweetly questioning
    If I lack'd anything.

"A guest," I answer'd, "worthy to be here."
    Love said, "you shall be he."
"I, the unkind, ungrateful? Ah, my dear,
    I cannot look on Thee."
Love took my hand and smiling did reply,
    "Who made the eyes but I?"

"Truth, Lord; but I have marr'd them: let my shame
    Go where it doth deserve."
"And know you not," says Love, "who bore the blame?"
    "My dear, then I will serve."
"You must sit down," says Love, "and taste my meat."
    So I did sit and eat.

Weil, like Herbert, did not distinguish among Christ, God/Lord, and Love. They are the same Person. The direct conversation in the poem, characteristic of other Herbert poems in *The Temple*, between the mortal poet, the guest, and the immortal Love/Lord takes place in the quiet of the room of the extraordinary visitation. The Lord and the priest/poet are alone, so they speak directly to each other, he of his unworthiness, unkindness, ingratitude, and shame and guilt. The Lord responds by reassuring the poet, explaining away the sins and then repeating the invitation.

    Surely the reader can feel the force of Herbert's words without my explication, especially the multilayered connotations of the last line. So powerful was the poem for Weil that it created the occasion of her second encounter with God, after Assisi.

I have not been so fortunate, having tried as Weil did to use the poem as mantra, as well as other poems I love, like Gerard Manley Hopkins's "Spring and Fall" and "I Wake and Feel the Dark." But still I learned valuable lessons from "Love": that possible encounters with God (or with the sense of Him) are private, not likely to take place during public worship, or that such an extraordinary meeting might occur after forgiveness for all my transgressions and the nonreception of sacramental food.

THE MIDDLE
OF THE ROAD

God clepe folk to hym in sondry ways . . .
—Geoffrey Chaucer, *The Canterbury Tales*
[Prologue, The Wife of Bath's Tale]

E T T A M A Y was an Indiana Quaker whose fine rule of life is mounted on our refrigerator:

> If thee needs
> Anything & cannot
> Find it,
> Just come to me
> And I'll tell thee
> How to get along
> Without it.

Fine for worldly goods, fame, food, elaborate homes, but not much help when I went in search of God. I knew I could not get along without Him.

THE WHITE BOOK

Dag Hammarskjöld's *Markings* came into my hands by chance just before the onset of shingles. Many people now alive will not know much about the remarkable statesman, but his was an extraordinary story. He was the son of a former prime minister of Sweden. He first served as chairman of the board of the Bank of Sweden, then as deputy foreign minister before being elected to the prestigious post of second secretary-general of the United

Nations. For eight years until his untimely and tragic death in a plane accident in Rhodesia (now Zambia) he was the most visible and active diplomat in the world, heading peace missions to the Middle East, the Orient, and Africa.

After his death his diary was found in his New York house. With it was a note, addressed to his friend, a diplomat at the U.N., in which he described the diary as "a sort of white book concerning my negotiations with myself—and with God." The diary was published in Sweden three years after his death (in 1961) and then published in English (with an intriguing, iconoclastic foreword by poet W. H. Auden) three years later.

Nowhere in the book, as Auden points out, is there a mention of DH's distinguished diplomatic career, his great worldly success. *Markings*, Auden notes, is not the work of a professional writer or a trained theological thinker but an account of "the attempt by a professional man of action to unite in one life the *via activa* and the *via contemplativa.*" DH believed, "In our era, the road to holiness necessarily passes through the world of action," a view that brought me to the thought that one way to a sense of God might be to move from action in the world to inaction in prayer. It was not so much a question of uniting the active and the contemplative world, as Auden thought, but the passage out of one into the other.

The Catholic humanitarian (some say "saint") Dorothy Day arrived at her kind of holiness on a path that at some point must have crossed DH's. She believed that "God is here and lives in all we do." For Auden the way had to be stricter. Being part of a worshiping community and relying on dogmatic theology was a necessity. He took Hammarskjöld to task for having a religion that was "more of a solitary and private thing than it should have been." Rather nervily, I thought, Auden felt sorry for him, regarding him as an introverted intellectual "who stands most in need of the ecclesiastic routine, both as a discipline and as a refreshment."

I knew it was a widely held belief that organized religion housed in a church is essential for the disciplined practice of one's faith. I knew it would be easier for me to subscribe to it. But what of the believer who found liturgical routine a barrier to prayer and the discipline of liturgy more a stopping place than a journey? The question brought me back from Auden's curious introduction to the healing paragraphs of Hammarskjöld's text.

DH wrote: "The more faithfully you listen to the voice within you, the better you will hear what is sounding outside. And only he who listens can speak." Once before, in a period of solitude, I learned that I had grown to love my family and friends better when I was alone. Now, reading the very early entries in his diary, I saw a valuable parallel to that lesson: what I have sometimes heard in periods of silence surrounding private prayer was an inner voice, undisguised by the obligations of conversation. Listening to it, *hearing* it, I was better able then to hear voices outside. DH knew the dangers of engaging in social talk "merely because convention forbids silence, to rub against one another in order to create the illusion of intimacy and contact; what an example of *la condition humaine.*"

Both realizations were further evidence to me of the value of solitude. To use it to strengthen my ties with the world made me feel less guilty about the pleasure I had come to take in it, in the deep joy of silence.

There remained the difficulty that too-great attentiveness to the inner voice would end in destructive solipsism. DH recognized that danger: "To reach perfection, we must all pass, one by one, through the death of self effacement." I was learning, when I prayed, or waited, or listened, that I could almost escape from the self, almost pass beyond it and, although perfection was not my goal, reach a place at which I would be ready "to sit and eat" if God's hospitality, as George Herbert described it, should be offered to me.

Lately, even living with pain, the best times alone were not static and immobile. I felt a small change in my self and my inner voice, a kind of developing and strengthening of the fibers that constitute the non-self. DH: "If only I may grow: firmer, simpler—quieter, warmer." The virtues of character (and is not character what the formed self displays in our worldly relations?) had begun to apply more to what I am within, that shadowy traveler on the unmarked path toward an absent God.

Often I wondered if I were wandering further and further from the reality of what was happening in the world—the news, the entertainments, the social gatherings, the births and deaths, the claims of progress and the need to understand technological "improvements"—in my pleasure at being removed from them all and inhabiting an inner universe. DH quotes (I don't know who): "For man shall commune with all creatures to his profit, but enjoy God alone."

DH wrote an answer to a question that I had been wrestling with since the beginnings of my first impatience with rite. "Prayer, crystallized in words, assigns a permanent wave length on which the dialogue has to be continued, even when our mind is occupied with other matters." I had been trying to escape the crystallization of prayer in words. It was a hard habit to break, so dependent was I on them, so sure that words alone would reach God's ears.

What was more, I had been wondering since I began the practice of private prayer whether I should keep track *in words* (how else?) of what I was finding, learning. DH encouraged me to separate my experience from any that I had heard or read about. "Only what is unique in a person's experience is worth writing down as a guide and a warning to others." Nonetheless, I decided to put it down, unique or not, as a test of its validity, as a reevaluation of the thinking and the nonthinking that have engrossed me.

DH kept a private diary. He was not concerned about possible readers, nor did he hope that he would have them. But at the end of his life he changed. His note to his friend about the diary seemed to indicate it might be worth publishing after his death. He had written in *Markings:* "It may be of interest to somebody to learn about a path about which the traveler who was committed to it did not wish to speak while he was alive." And he added: "Perhaps—but only if what you write has an honesty with no trace of vanity or self-regard." Beware, I thought, be very careful that this be so.

The writer of *Markings* was a lonely man with no close family and, seemingly, few close friends. He was a career diplomat with great social gifts, who wrote:

> Congenial to other people?
> It is with yourself
> That you must live.

He was an occasional poet—the diary begins and ends with a poem. Most of the poems were written during the last three years of his life. But I suspect that literature did not appear to him to be suitable for a man of action, so he confined his poetry to another, spiritual sphere. He lived a secret religious life, writing of his spiritual discoveries once he had said *"Yes* to God."

He was a man called upon to make hundreds of speeches to international audiences, yet he thought that "the best and most wonderful thing that can happen to you in this life is that you should be silent and let God work and speak." Required to appear on numerous world stages on behalf of suffering humanity, reconciliation, and peace, he wrote, close to the end of his life: "Only when you descend into yourself and encounter the Other, do you experience goodness as the ultimate reality—united and living—*in* Him and *through* you."

Despite the pain that hiding his real self must have cost him, and the suffering that came from disguises, masks, loneliness, and doubt, he wrote, in the year of his death, that he had found God. "At some moment I did answer *Yes* to Someone—or Something—and from that hour I was certain that existence is meaningful and that, therefore, my life, in self-surrender, has a goal."

DH was a guide, a trustworthy helping hand on my journey. What was more, in his prose and poetry he provided me with other names for God: the Other, Someone, Something, Thee: "Thou / Whom I do not know / But Whose I am."

FEEL A JOY

Edward Kessler, a good friend from the days of academe in Washington, came to visit, bringing a new book by a country doctor. In it David Lexterkamp recounted, month by month, his life of ser-

vice to his patients. He had kept a journal which served as text for
A Measure of My Days, and had been reading Kathleen Norris's
books. Like hers, his conclusion differed from mine. He wrote: "I
can now confirm in my own life what Kathleen Norris discovered on the South Dakota plains: living in community is the only
asceticism you need."

I could not argue with this view—so true for him and for so
many others. But what I found difficult to accept was the hard
sound of absolute judgment in it: it is the *only* way to go, the doctor said. Social action, service, community, fellowship, were the
designated paths that bring the seeker to God, not the single-file
progress into the interior I had been trying to make.

Somewhere I read that Meister Eckhart, the thirteenth-
century Dominican monk, said: "A man can only spend in good
works what he earns in contemplation."

I wondered if perhaps it was a question of age. When my energy
and ambition were high, my vision was fixed on what, with the
easy activity of a healthy, well-functioning body, I might do in
the world. In age, however, I have come away from that reliance
and have begun to live almost entirely within. There, undisturbed by the clamor and activity I once loved, I hoped to encounter in the privacy of that small inner core the Presence I yearned
for.

As if to make up for introducing me to the contrary (to mine)
conclusions of Dr. Lexterkamp, Ed sent me a list of Emily Dickinson's poems that he thought might encapsulate my personal
leanings. I liked #875 (in *The Complete Poems*):

> I stepped from Plank to Plank
> A slow and cautious way

The Stars about my Head I felt
About my Feet the Sea.

I knew not but the next
Would be my final inch—
This gave me that precarious Gait
Some call Experience.

Dickinson was a lifelong recluse, a poet who found all the subject matter she needed within herself, like the legendary spider who pulls her web with her chelicerae from her breast. "In many and reportless places / We feel a Joy—" she writes in #1382. In those lines I thought I heard a reproach. Perhaps my use of the "Joy" on the Millwood steps would have been better off unreported. But I took heart at her final words: "Profane it by a search—we cannot / It has no home—/ Nor we who having once inhaled it—/ Thereafter roam."

I continued to be surprised by how much writers long dead have taught me. "Whose I am," and "We feel a Joy,"—words to use for meditation. I began to feel it necessary to extend, to expand upon, the one-word prayer I had been using, to set aside for some time to come the old hope that repetition would serve to establish its absolute meaning, as saying a word over and over often does, until the moment when it disappears into the nothingness. Too often this happened when I waited for Whose I am.

LUTHER, MATTHEW, WEIL

"It is impossible for one who prays spiritually (not through obedience or for the sake of gain) to be verbose," Martin Luther wrote in an essay on the Lord's Prayer. He was an early advocate of minimalism in prayer. "Those who pray least seem to pray most, and conversely, those who pray most seem to pray least."

Luther quoted St. Jerome's story of a holy man who lived in the desert. For thirty years, it was said, he carried a stone in his mouth in order to teach himself silence. Luther wondered how he prayed and decided, "Without a doubt, inwardly with his heart." Luther was hard on the spoken words of prayer. "They have no other purpose than that of a trumpet, a drum or an organ." He concluded his instructions to one who prayed, urging him to beware of words "mumbled and uttered with the mouth" until such time as he was able to "fly without the help of words."

Saint Matthew too was suspicious of verbosity. "No one will be heard just because he uses many words." He was harsh toward those he called hypocrites, those who insisted on praying in public "so that they may be seen by others." His instruction on how to pray is detailed: "Go into your room and shut the door and pray to your Father who is in secret." He urges upon them the Lord's Prayer, an exact formulation from Matthew which Christians have accepted and have prayed for two thousand years. It is not an especially terse prayer, so it has provided material for a great number of works of exegesis, few of them as cogent and rewarding as Simone Weil's.

It was from Weil in *Concerning the Lord's Prayer* that I learned a way to make that oft-repeated prayer more meaningful. She had memorized it in Greek and repeated it over and over again as she worked in a vineyard harvesting grapes: "The infinite sweetness of this Greek text . . . took hold of me."

Πάτερ ἡμῶν ὁ ἐν τοῖς οὐρανοῖς

My Greek was very rusty, but I thought I would try it, to give new life to the prayer that in English had been deadened for me by repetition. I found it too difficult to memorize the Greek, so I kept the text in hand, dwelling on each word, as Weil did "with absolutely pure attention."

It astonished me to discover the new richness, the variant meanings the Greek words suggested to me. Some mornings it took me fifteen minutes to pray in this language. At other times I stopped at the first words, Πάτερ ἡμῶν, and said them again and again. I found a texture there that strangely enough led me back into my square, despairing that nothing, no sense of God, had arrived. Still, I was willing to wait, remembering what I had read in *Beginning to Pray*, Anthony Bloom's book of instruction for prayer. "The day when God is absent, when he is silent—that is the beginning of prayer."

I tried to understand why it is that praying in another language brings new significance to the prayer. I decided that words in one's own language harden in time. They seem to have been connotative in youth, but slowly they lose all their overtones (and undertones), become indurate and denotative, and then often, with repetition, pass through the mind without leaving very much of an impression.

But when the sound changes, a new set of connotations appear. I thought I might go back to the now-abandoned Latin *Pater Noster* I once said so glibly to see if new import would occur to me, or to the French I knew less well, or to the Spanish I had almost completely forgotten. I was intoxicated by the thought of endless possibilities, awash in them. This was a retreat, I then realized, a

moving backward into the power of language. So I returned to
Our Father, vowing not to use linguistic tricks to advance my
search. "One does not seek for God, one waits for him." (Simone
Weil again.) I would wait.

THE SAINT'S DISEASE

Ellen LeConte, who is writing a life of Helen Nearing, the guru of
the back-to-the-land movement, sent me a package full of good
reading matter. I found in Kimon Friar's introduction to Nikos
Kazantzakis's *The Saviors of God* a description of NK's curious
affliction which came upon him after an evening spent at the Vi-
enna Opera. It was a kind of eczema which "spread from his lips
and chin, mounted to his eyes and forehead. Soon all his face had
puffed up until his eyes were pinpoints in a loathsome blubber of
flesh. His lower lip, swollen to many times its normal size,
dripped with a peculiar kind of yellow liquid."

Aha, I thought. NK's affliction was like mine, only situated, as
is common, on another area of the body. Friar reported that there
was nothing in medicine that helped him. So NK resorted to a
well-known psychiatrist, Wilhelm Stekel, who questioned him
about his recent activities. NK told him he had met a beautiful
woman one night at the opera after which his facial disfigure-
ment had come upon him. Immediately Dr. Stekel diagnosed the
trouble as what he called "the saint's disease." In the Middle
Ages, he said, men who aspired to holiness went to the desert or
into caves to atone for their sins and to free their bodies of the
temptations of the flesh. Those who could not bear the solitude
gave up and went back to town to find women. On their way, they

broke out in terrible sores and boils; "a yellow liquid dripped from their pores."

Dr. Stekel advised Kazantzakis, who, he said, was trying to live as a holy man in another century and so was suffering similarly, to give up all thoughts of the lady, in fact to leave the city. His instruction was effective. As soon as NK stepped on the train for Berlin, his swellings disappeared.

I was struck by this account. I wondered if it could be that I too had been afflicted by the saint's disease, not because I had tried for purity and sainthood but because I had begun to worship in a private way, to wait for the Ineffable alone. NK had moved from his experience with affliction to a search for a genuine spirituality. He wrote: "I have one longing only: to grasp what is hidden behind appearances . . . to discover if behind the visible and unceasing stream of the world an invisible, an immutable presence is hiding." And: "What is my duty? . . . to let the mind fall silent that I may hear the Invisible calling."

To let the mind fall silent is the hardest thing I have ever tried to do. And yet, in moments of blankness and deep silence it is just possible that my search, echoed in the Psalmist's cry, will be answered, out of a pillar of cloud (99:7), from the mouth of a hidden God (143:1–7). In Kathleen Norris's *The Cloister Walk* I learned that Gregory of Nyssa wrote that Moses "entered the darkness and then saw God in it."

LETTER

Dear Kathleen Norris: Nothing I have read in the last three years has fired me up as much as *Dakota* and then *The Cloister Walk*.

Your stories and references have been most useful, but more than that, you have provided me with sticking points for my questions, the hard places against which I could rub my theories, my recent discoveries. I admired your descriptions of the beauty you found on the bare plains of South Dakota after the excitements of the stimulating, jangled city.

You wrote (in *Dakota*) that the literary drought, the deprivations and "separateness" of the plains, had taught you better to accept strangers and crowds in the city and drew you "to the monastery." I understood this, although somehow I had managed to skip the middle step. I went from years of the city life I feared and distrusted to the seclusion of the cove in Sargentville without learning to accept the crowds and noise.

It is not merely a matter of age. A young English writer I had been reading left the city permanently because, she said, she could not "afford to live in a place that cannot afford silence." Nothing in my blessed, newfound quiet had taught me to see, as you say Merton found, that "it is the function of solitude . . . that teaches me that when I am in the city there are no strangers . . . and that the gate of heaven is everywhere."

Odd, isn't it, that solitude had made me grateful for the absence of the city and then unable "to see God in all things," to see very little evidence of Him in the clamor and crash and confusion of the city.

I liked the story at the end of the chapter entitled "Deserts." "A brother came to Scetis to visit Abba Moses and asked him for a word. The old man said to him, 'Go, sit in your cell, and your cell will teach you everything.'" For some reason it was the fact of the smallness of the monastic cell rather than its all-inclusiveness that struck me. I found I could pray more successfully on our small porch than on the more expansive deck. There, too much space made it hard to move down and into my field of interior vision.

We are alike in our need to find a place in which to approach God, and yet how different are our ways of conducting the search. Even more, we've started on the journey from opposite departure points. You write about being religious in early childhood and coming from a family of religious persons ("Religion is in my blood, and in my ghosts," you say). For a long time that familial inheritance was lost on you until, *mirabile*, you came back to faith in your beloved Benedictine monastery.

How strange it seemed to me that for you and, I am sure, for most people religion was best learned in community, that "communal worship is something I need." Our differences lie in both origin and place. I had no such heritage, no faith in my blood, no holy ghosts hovering about me. I *had* one heart-churning "experience," which I now think of as an epiphany, that sent me into half a century of vain attempts to re-create it in communal worship. At last, despairing of that path, I tried to enter that most monastic of places, the inner cell of the self.

I was interested in your description of an almost-silent retreat you once attended. You tell of the more than one hundred women from various professions who came together in the monastery in North Dakota to "try to strike a balance between the active and contemplative life." There you discovered that "to live communally in silence is to admit a new power into your life."

I wondered, Why did the presence of so many persons maintaining an almost contemplative silence in community impress you so powerfully? Starting from an opposite point, and having never made a communal retreat, I wondered if the coming together of many persons to pray in silence would work as well for me as my silent waiting in solitude, undisturbed and undistracted, surrounded by no sounds but my own breathing and the occasional cawing of crows in the meadow.

Somewhere in *The Cloister Walk* (which I read with equal pleasure) you used the term "hermitage retreat." I wondered if that was an oxymoron, or if retreat could mean retreat for one, rather than the current suggestion of gathering with others for what to me has come to require solitude. But perhaps I have misinterpreted it. I remember being surprised when a nun-friend once said to me, "We are all going on retreat."

As I wrote this I thought, perhaps a retreat in this sense is the halfway house to true solitude. My difficulties with private prayer after a half century of public worship might have been eased if I had made a less abrupt transition. I remember that when I told my rector, Allan, of my new way he suggested I try a retreat at his monastery of choice in Massachusetts.

But my method—to plunge into the cold waters of silent singularity without preparation—was the way I took. I was searching for a renewal, a reoccurrence of the sense of the Sacred which I had lost by the end of my church-going. I have always been one to approach change in my life radically, never gradually. I remembered that Thomas Merton left the world to become a Trappist monk and then, finding he needed more solitude than the monastery provided, built himself a solitary hut in the woods. His was a gradualist's approach to private prayer. I am curious whether you will come to it eventually, whether for you it will always be true, especially as you grow older, that liturgy will, instead, feed and embody your faith but will act as the doorway into the increasing privacy of the self.

Ralph Waldo Emerson said he enjoyed "the silence in a church before the service more than any sermon."

I have gone on long enough. I want to ask you much more about your observations and findings in *Cloister*, but I will wait for another time. I am grateful for the stimulus I have found so far.

THE MYSTERIOUS SACRED

In *The Temple in the House* the architect Anthony Lawlor writes:

> The sacred cannot be precisely defined. Each of us perceives it through the lens of a unique personal history. For me, sacredness is an experience of the inner radiance of life, the unseen force that transforms and nourishes the physical world but is never limited by it. There is something more to it, a mystery that is never totally grasped.

The book's subtitle is "Finding the sacred in everyday architecture," a subject I had never thought about. But Lawlor's words suggested that my search for a reencounter with the Sacred (should I now give this name to what I once felt?) might have been too limited. I wanted to retrieve what for one moment I knew in precisely the shape (lessness?) it had then. Ought I to have looked less deeply, more widely? Had I been searching in only one place, the inner, blank square, without attending to the vast array of the ordinary outside myself?

The mystery of the Sacred that is never grasped: must I surrender my hope of a precise Encounter to the Mystery that will never be understood, never encountered in the same way, in the same place, in the same shape again? For once I was tempted to abandon my narrow corner, my one-word or wordless prayer, my daily, slow trudge back through the layers of the fleshly self to the empty square at the core, and to the wait.

But the next morning I returned to my old practice, to the music of silence (the title of David Steindl-Rast's book on singing the Psalms), and to the contemplation of lines in Psalm 105:4: "Search for the Lord and his strength. / Continually seek his face"; and then the usual long, silent wait.

THOMAS KELLY, QUAKER

During these two years I had grown, reluctantly, in the conviction that the longer I waited, the harder I looked, the less sure I was that I would be able to recapture that first, astonishing time. If the Sacred cannot be "precisely defined" or caught hold of in any way, then the certainty with which I had embarked on my journey was reduced to nothing.

At the peak of my despair someone gave me a Quaker "tract" (do they still call such pamphlets that?) by Thomas Kelly, a writer who died, very young, in 1941. To come upon *A Testament of Devotion* was a serendipitous encounter, the discovery in print of a sensibility so tuned to my despondency that I found myself engrossed in a new and nourishing view.

Kelly never spoke of seeking God, a Presence always beyond, always out of man's grasp or comprehension, but instead of finding God within that inner space which, to me, had always seemed empty when I prayed, Kelly's view was that one's life is layered: the secular level on which all the business of life is carried on, and the deeper, important layer where what he termed "the Light" is, "where the soul ever dwells in the presence of the Holy One."

If his locus is not outside ourselves, then my search had been misdirected. I used to take "who art in Heaven" literally. Kelly wanted to point me in another direction, to deep within myself where God may reside. He warned me that the practice of communication with God is hard and time-consuming. While Kelly's verbiage was awkward his meaning was clear: "Even years must be passed through before He gives us greater and easier stayedness upon Himself." One must pass through the layer of worldliness and then "surrender to Him who is within."

It may be that, despairingly, I had been hungering for God because to my blind eyes He was always absent, or because my vision was directed to some futile point beyond me, outside. Kelly wrote: "Admit no discouragement but ever return quietly to Him and *wait in His Presence*" (italics are mine). The wait that was accompanied; I was heartened by the thought.

Kelly saw worldly concerns as a detriment to the secret, hidden prayer life, together with pride in learning (theology and church history are the subjects he mentioned) and "much of the external trappings of religion." His method of prayer was that of the early mystics whose profound mystical experience was "to be invaded to the depths of one's being by His presence."

He described the same essential elements that contemplatives such as Meister Eckhart and Thomas Merton knew about: movement from the complex to the simple, from verbalization to what "you meant the words to say." Kelly urged that we assume "attitudes of self-abandonment," during which "all we can say is, Prayer is taking place, and I am given to be in the orbit." When the true place within is located, and when words are given up, then "one stands and walks and sits and lies in wordless attitudes of adoration and submission and rejoicing and exaltation and glory."

All this made encouraging reading, but my two-year-long practice had brought me nowhere close to a wonderful fulfillment of this kind. However, Thomas Kelly warned of the difficulties, instructing me that God educates us "by means of dryness as well as by means of glory."

What I was learning in my difficult practice of contemplative prayer was that serenity, a deep calm, often came to me, supplanting my expectation of ecstasy and replacing my hope of a direct experience of God, or a sense of God, as I believed I had once known it. I was in want, in need. Still, I had learned that the hunger for God must be accompanied by long patience, by the trials of despair, and fed, in my case at least, by ineluctable pain.

Near the end of his life Thomas Kelly wrote that he had learned a lesson: We must live in "a God-directed mode of being." The manuscript, published after his death, was called "Hasten unto God." This rush was to be made first; and after that one could move into the suffering world. He seemed to have lost faith in the efficacy of worldly service, even in the church which "by its weakness and supine worldliness, shows desperate need of its radical reorientation, and fundamentally its rediscovery that religion is *primarily* built around God . . . not around the world."

In the weeks I spent with Thomas Kelly's books I found myself strongly in sympathy with his Quaker views. If I was not a Quietist, perhaps I was, in theory at least, a Quaker, a believer that the first step in prayer had to be away from the world and the final stopover the locus in God. I was caught and held by his distrust of religion when it becomes luxury, or "fancy work for the idle rich," or secular.

I had discovered how necessary it was (for me) to discard my stale concepts of God and ritual practices in order to approach the pure core of prayer. A long life in the church had formed me into a halfhearted, secular worshiper. It was this condition I had to cast off. Kelly led me back and then beyond what I had tried to write to Allan. Kelly writes:

> For when we, in actual practice, only know God by hearsay, and pay Him traditional deference, and when we rely chiefly upon our heads, upon our *economic* information, and upon our *political* shrewdness and our *social* skill to reconstruct the world, we are *secular.*

I had been just that kind of worshiper, reading about God, talking about Him in intellectual and philosophical terms and so relegating Him to the outskirts of my interesting and active life. God had been put into a convenient time, an aesthetically pleasing place. I had taken the much-traveled, highly populated, secular and socially acceptable road toward Him. I think I feared the solitary trek, feared to desert the safe highway for what others might consider a mad, egocentric excursion. But Kelly reassured me: "Better to run the possible risk of fanaticism by complete dedication to God than to run the certain risk of mediocrity by twenty-percent dedication."

Finally, before I put his two books back on the shelf, I mulled over what at first, in my early pursuit of a sense of God, seemed so, well, *crazy* but which now had taken on the semblance of soul-saving sanity. Into my journal I copied out Kelly's sentence: "But then comes crucial periods in life when the quest for God grows hot, when the hot breath of the Hound of Heaven is at our heels, when the heart cries out, 'Give me the Presence or I die.'"

At these moments, I understood, we leave behind "the conventional mildness of average religiosity" and enter the inner desert of the self where the hot sands scorch our feet and the burning sun makes us foolish and hot for God.

LETTER FROM KEATS

The poet John Keats wrote to his brothers in the beginning of the nineteenth century a gossipy letter about seeing Edmund Kean, the most famous actor of his time, in a performance of *Richard III*. Then he said he had gone to see a painting by Benjamin West (the American painter) called *Death on a Pale Horse.* These visits led him to speculate that "the excellence of every art is its intensity" (a truth that Henry James reiterated much later when he said a novel was to be judged not by its subject matter but by the intensity with which it was projected).

Keats went on to characterize men of achievement in literature, especially William Shakespeare. Their essential quality was "*Negative* Capability," that which marks a man "capable of being with uncertainties, Mysteries, doubts, without any irritable reaching after fact & reason."

It struck me that, with some stretching, these terms could be used to describe a quality accepted by persons immersed in contemplative prayer. For there is always much more doubt than certainty, never any facts, and always so much ambiguity. One must be willing to live with uncertainties, indeed to embrace them, because that is all one has. Immersed in doubts, one must fight against despair. To encounter the sense of God again was, for me, a dubious expectation, given the mysteries of existence and the strong possibility that such a meeting might not take place. Always reason argued with me about the whole enterprise, and only negative capability and the intensity of my hope kept me at prayer.

LETTER TO WALTER

My friend, you raised good questions. You asked about my description of the Experience, "How did I know who It was?" Then you queried me further. "Do you say that who It was became self-evident at some point? Or did you have to decide, in yourself, at some point, who you *believed* It was?" It was first a temporal query: *when* did I know; and then a theoretical one: where was the line drawn between belief and knowledge?

The more I thought about it over the years the more curious it seemed that I *knew* (there never was doubt, always certainty) at once, at that point, on the spot, as they say. Further, never was it a question of *believing. I knew.* It was curious, unique to my rational way of thinking, for never again that I could recall had I been so certain of anything. Then there was no negative capability. *I knew,* beyond doubts and uncertainties. Still, ambiguity hovered on the edge and the mystery of it continued to haunt me for almost fifty years. But yet, I knew.

Walter, you have widened my view that the Psalms are descriptions of the constant wars with political enemies of Israel or of the inner spiritual battles within the Psalmist himself. You paraphrased a commentator on Psalm 137 who thought that "the significant theological virtue of the Psalm which asks God to take angry and retributive action against the outside world may be that the prayer was relinquishing the handling of these evildoers to God, rather than taking it on themselves."

This is an interesting view, with its emphasis on the independent actions of the Lord rather than the interior struggle within the soul. Perhaps the answer lies in further subdividing the kinds of Psalms there are (as Robert Alter ordered them) to include Psalms of Struggle Within the Self (my category), and Psalms that assign retributive action to the Lord.

Another matter: I remember our talk over lunch one day about how far "the body" of the church extended. Your feeling was that there was a certain "tyranny" in the thought that "one size fits all." You assured me that wherever I now stood, on the threshold like Simone Weil, or in the privacy of the room in which I prayed, I belonged to the body in the deepest sense. Departure from the liturgy was not, you wrote, a barrier. "The liturgy, important as it is to many of us and, in some senses, to all of us, must never become something from which we cannot detach ourselves," you said.

You question whether it is possible for anyone to know "the pure love of God." Good Lord, did I ever say I hoped to know it? I must have, or you would not be questioning me. I rarely if ever associate "love" with what I am seeking to recapture or experience again. I have avoided the word because it seemed presumptuous to me. I wanted to sense God's presence, but I found it very hard to believe He loved me, or returned my affection for Him. Purity of anything, especially love, is an absolute I have never believed in.

Another thing: like you, I do not believe it is possible or necessary "to escape the created world in which God has placed us." I know this to be true, although it is also true that I try to avoid the world of persons as often as I can. But surely the world is there, in the store and the post office, in the restaurant and the room in which guests and relatives sit, in letters, in phone calls, and on the radio and, glaringly, in the newspaper. The world feels as close to me as an outer skin; I cannot escape it.

But for me, in contemplative prayer, it is a different matter. I succeed to the degree that I can shed *at that moment* all connection to the world and its people. I do not try this during the rest of my day. I could not if I wanted to; I have not been granted the luxury of living as a hermit.

I understand you when you say that you "put a lot of stock in a doctrine of the Incarnation which holds that God comes to us and, therefore, is accessible to us in other human beings, that God is otherness as well as closeness . . . immanence as well as transcendence." How well I know the truth of your saying that "we are stuck with/in our humanity." It is useless, even for a few moments a day, to make a temporary escape. This transient touching of the spirit (do you notice how seldom I use this word? Like "love," I suppose, it is easy verbiage to the tongue but very difficult to define or understand) is a small step toward God. And once I move in this way it is hard to turn back to humanity.

Thomas Merton wrote on a somewhat different subject but

about the same sort of progress: "Once God has called you to solitude, everything you touch leads you further into solitude.
Everything that affects you builds you into a hermit, as long as
you do not insist on doing the work yourself and building your
own kind of hermitage."

"As long as you do not insist upon. . . . " The warning here is
clear and disturbs me now that I have reread it. Am I insisting on
my own way so heavily that I have eliminated the possibilities
that lie in all the others? Have I made too strict a dichotomy between community and solitude (self, perhaps?), between public
and the private worship?

I take to heart your suggestion that these idiosyncratic choices
of mine are a function of age, not of knowledge or of experience.
In old age the rhythmic movement of life that Henri Nouwen
speaks of seems (for me, at least) to have halted in solitude. It is
not necessarily more salutary, as you say, than community, but
at this late date I am more needful of it.

THE NUMBER OF DAYS

The Psalmist said first: "There is no health in my flesh . . . there
is no soundness in my body (because of my sin)" (38:3). Four lines
later (v. 7) in the same Psalm he repeated: "There is no health in
my body," having earlier confessed: "I have been young, and now
I am old" (37:26). In many of the Psalms the outcries, petitions,
threats of revenge, hymns of praise and admissions of failure, pro-
tests against desertion and loneliness, the despairing admissions
of unbridgeable distance from God seem to be the predictable
clamorings of an old person.

It is so for me. Always now the real challenge is accepting the limitations of old age. What once seemed possible now seems less (and less) likely to happen in the time left. This is not simply the usual, deepening pessimism about everything in old age but the acute and troubling sense that time is giving out in which I could be visited again by the sense of God. The poet Philip Larkin described his dread of dying:

> But at the total emptiness for ever,
> The sure extinction that we travel to
> And shall be lost in always. Not to be here.
> Not to be anywhere,
> And soon; nothing more terrible, nothing more true.

"Most things may never happen: this one will," he wrote, and I thought of my dread that the one thing I wanted to happen again, the one Encounter, would never happen; only "sure extinction," only that.

The Psalmist mourned: "For my days drift away like smoke / and my bones are hot as burning coals" (102:3).

For me (although I know that, for many others, this is not so) old age is the darkening night of the soul. The despairing Psalmist asked the Lord, with perhaps that same sense of little time left: "O when will you come to me?" (102:2). Old age is the dim pillar of cloud in which bodily infirmity increases and the smoke of drifting days threatens to obscure the limited horizon. Could it be that it was an old person whom God "led . . . with a cloud by day" (78:14), the same one who lamented: "My life is at the brink of the grave" (88:3) and then asked God to "teach us to number our days" (90:12).

When I combined the thought of the final number of my days with the pain that now occupied them, I recognized the pit into which the Psalmist had sunk: "Out of the depths have I called to you, O Lord" (131:1). Meister Eckhart, on the contrary, in *The Essential Sermons*, spoke of suffering as "the fastest beast that will carry you to your perfection." He was aware that "nothing disfigures the body more than suffering . . . and nothing more adorns the soul in the sight of God than to have suffered."

At moments of greatest pain, I thought about death. Living close to the sea, and reading Hermione Lee's superb biography of Virginia Woolf, I contemplated finding a stone for my pocket and walking into the water. I shared Philip Larkin's terror of death and obliteration, but the thought of living on with intractable pain was even more terrible. Once I came very close to making that escape, as in the words of Psalm 142:6: "for I have been brought very low." But I remembered Dag Hammarskjöld saying: "Do not seek death. Death will find you. But seek the road which makes death a fulfilment."

I resolved to reconsider the uses of pain, to cut deep into the blank, silent core of self where wordless prayer flourishes, and not to dwell any longer on the means to obliterate it. As long as I could find some use for it I would permit it to occupy me. Regarded in this way I saw how far I had advanced from my old, lifelong use of thoughtless prayer as "a nice, pious duty," in Karl Barth's derogatory words. I would offer no petitions for health or the release from constant pain. I knew Anthony Bloom was right when he observed, "When we pray, we want something from Him, not Him at all." I wanted God, or the sense of Him. I did not wish to waste the time still allotted to me on anything less.

My wearying solemnity toward myself and my avid pursuit was on occasion dispelled by small, funny thoughts. At one point I told friends I would have my shingles surgically removed and replace them with vinyl siding. More useful, I decided to resort to witchcraft and accept pain as a familiar, to be with me always, a severe, inseparable companion.

At first this was a joke. But the more I thought about it, the more useful the concept of a familiar became. Pain and suffering might be accepted not as an injustice done to my sound body, not as something the healthy self did not deserve to have (Why *me?*), but a predictable and inevitable ingredient of an aged body. It might even be that it was not within but something hovering close by, as the *Oxford English Dictionary* has it, a spirit that is always attentive when one calls, always "there for you," in contemporary idiom.

Lord Byron, I read somewhere, saw emotion as an inescapable familiar, to be dispelled only when life ended. "Twelve days had Fear been their familiar, and now Death was here." Death was the unfamiliar. So, I thought I would give pain the role of familiar, and be reconciled to it at the approach of the unfamiliar.

WRITING ABOUT PRAYER

To have told someone about what I intended to write was, I knew, to lose it entirely or destroy it. Never in the past did I discuss a book or an idea until I had safely committed it to paper. Now I was to learn that to write about the experience of contemplative prayer while I was still learning to practice it was to interfere with the act. Writing introduced the intrusive self into the waiting room, creating a curtain of prose that obscured the desired purity of the prayer. Any small event occupied space in the necessary period of emptiness—a stray thought, a cramp in the foot, a high-flying osprey over the sky of the cove. The act of writing became the most distracting.

But then I was saved; I read that Franz Kafka had written somewhere: "Writing is a form of prayer."

THE CLOUD OF UNKNOWING

Most useful to me as guide was an anonymous monk who wrote in the fourteenth century. He was a contemporary of Geoffrey Chaucer, Julian of Norwich, and other English mystics such as Richard Rolle. Little is known about the monk except that he was twenty-four years old (he tells us in his text), lived in an English monastery, was far enough along in the practice of contemplative prayer to advise his fellow monks, and translated into Middle English an extraordinary work, *Hidden Divinity*, by an early-sixth-century Syriac monk, Dionysius the Areopagite.

The doctrine of the English monk in *The Cloud of Unknowing* is close to that of Dionysius, whom the monk calls Denis. They believed that reason and mystical contemplation are both possible ways to God, the latter being the better way. Denis calls it "mystical" or "hidden," in that God can be known to human beings only negatively. What God is *not* (in shape or in any other way we may conceive of Him or think He acts) is the best way we can know Him. God is a "divine darkness," or in the fine title of Denis's book, a hidden divinity.

Negativity is allied with emptiness, *is* emptiness, the absence of positive content. Meister Eckhart wrote: "And you must know that to be empty of all created things is to be full of God, and to be full of created things is to be empty of God." I took these observations to heart because of the continuing wait for God in my prayers, because of the cloud of unknowing in which I existed.

The English monk told his fellows that there were four steps of growth during which they could exercise their "lively longing for God." Begin at the Common, or everyday manner of Christian life "along with your friends." Proceed to the Special manner, to the desire for which God awakens you, thence to the Singular where you "live the interior life more perfectly," and finally to the Perfect, which is a matter of highest desire, not to be fulfilled until after death.

He, like Denis, instructed those wishing to know God to be resigned to a long darkness, a cloud of the mind, where God may rarely be encountered, deep in "this darkness of unknowing that lies between you and your God."

What a comfort a largely negative view of my enterprise was, how good to be told that there was no positive, inevitable, reassuring, exact way to a sense of God. "You are powerless to grasp him. Be still," he tells his fellow monks. There it was again: *Be still.* Like his, mine was to be a secret, silent, motionless pursuit, a race without steps, a desire without the promise of fulfillment. I was grateful for this reassurance. It is a matter of wish: "a naked intent toward God, a desire for him alone is enough."

Throughout his book, the English monk speaks of contemplative prayer as "work." For me this was true. Exercising the powers of reason is easy, but does not serve; it is futile to resort to it. As Keats thought in another connection, living with uncertainty and doubt rather than reaching for fact and reason is the true climate of contemplative work.

I was interested in the monk's one paragraph on liturgical worship in church, a way of prayer "for which the true contemplative has the highest esteem." True, he says, it preserves the traditions of the past, and we must be careful and exact in celebrating it, but it has little to do with the contemplative's personal, private prayer which is "wholly spontaneous." Having made a dutiful obeisance to public observance, he, like Merton in *Contemplative Prayer*, never mentions it again.

God, hitherto hidden in the cloud of unknowing, may come to you "like a sudden intuition," an "obscure certainty." It is His gift, wholly gratuitous, never earned, and only achieved by means of "great anguish." When it happens "it becomes your whole life." A light will pierce the cloud, the monk says, and then he abandons any attempt to describe it further: "The experience is beyond words."

His view of the uses of sickness (how often have I looked for help with this) was not of much assistance. Do not, he tells his listeners, stop praying because of it. But it is a good idea to avoid being sick (at this I gasped) because contemplative work "demands a relaxed, healthy, and vigorous disposition of both body and spirit." But if, try as you might, you are sick, bear your affliction with patience. Grow accustomed to practicing long, dark patience because such a virtue may be "more pleasing to God than tender feelings of devotion in times of health."

At that moment, to keep from becoming preoccupied with pain, I read *A Canticle for Leibowitz* by William Miller. I came to the place in the novel where a priest tells a woman with a sick child that pain is not pleasing to God (another of those times when I wondered how anyone could know this).

> It is the soul's endurance in faith and hope and love *in spite of* bodily afflictions that pleases Heaven. Pain is like negative temptation. God is not pleased by temptation that afflicts the flesh; He is pleased when the soul rises above the temptation. . . . It's the same with pain, which is often a temptation to despair, anger, loss of faith.

And then he assured the woman that "even the ancient pagans noticed that Nature imposes nothing on you that Nature doesn't prepare you to bear."

Seated in the half-dark of an early morning in the spring, full of resentment at hurting so much, unable to summon up even a modicum of patience to endure it, I finished the English monk's book of instructions. What stayed in my mind as I began once again to try to pray was his quotation from St. John of the Cross in *The Living Flame of Love:* "A short prayer pierces the heavens."

"God," I said into the silence of the dawn, and deeper, into the blank square in my mind. There was no answer, but then, I had become accustomed to living in a cloud of unknowing.

ABSENCE/PRESENCE

There were times during the years of my apprenticeship to contemplative prayer when I found meaning in books that seemed at first to be far from my sphere of interest. Walter suggested I read James Hillman's chapter on "growth" in his book *Kinds of Power,* written for businessmen and intended to instruct them in the intelligent uses of power. Hillman outlined a number of kinds of growth (deepening, intensification, shedding, repetition) and then came to "emptying," most interesting to me because I was engaged in that activity for different reasons. I was not concerned with succeeding in business but in understanding how the act of emptying could contribute to growth in the practice of contemplative prayer.

Goethe, Hillman said, examined leaf growth and decided that a plant's shape was somehow decided "by the negative space around which the leaves unfold. . . . Something in the surrounding emptiness governs the leaf's shaping." Like Goethe, Hillman was interested in what is not there, which, curiously, determined the nature of each leaf. "Emptiness has an invisible power that plays a determining role in what appears."

All this sounded idiosyncratic to me, hard to accept, until he reached a point that I found useful to my crooked way of thinking. He referred to Buddhist theory in which it is believed that seeds are held in a substratum void and "care for emptiness is what allows the seed to emerge." And then, even more intriguing (for me): "Absence takes precedence over presence, or better said, is the first form of presence."

Ah. So, if it is true that absence is the first form of presence, clearly my cloud of unknowing may some day contain God's presence. The emptiness of my present prayer, perhaps, may shape His appearance if the sense of God should ever arrive. And what is best of all, the seed planted in me on the Millwood steps might sprout into a prescribed shape, a Presence determined by long absence.

FARRAGO

Into a messy heap on one side of my desk I had the habit of tossing bits of paper containing thoughts and quotations I had collected during the past feverish two years. Sometimes I pulled one out and developed it into extended paragraphs, even chapters. One day in a fit of tidiness I decided to reduce the pile, recording their contents in these pages and then throwing the rest away. These scraps remain:

▨ Steve Jacobsen, writing in *Hearts to God, Hands to Work*: "The spiritual quest does not mean that the 'external world' is not real or is without value; instead it allows us to see our proper relationship with it. Our task . . . is to work with each other to penetrate the illusions, uncover the presence of the living God, and live together in response to grace."

Real: a problematic word. Here it was applied to the external world. But I shared Merton's view in his journals: "The reality of my life is the reality of interior prayer always and above all." He was increasingly dubious about what could be gained by joining groups. In recording in his fourth *Journal* the visit of a priest who was planning a "workshop" (the quotation marks are Merton's), he wrote: "The whole thing seems to me a little unreal. . . . I find it hard to attach importance to 'getting together and talking.'"

Where did I go for instruction? To talk with others? To gather in seminars, classes, workshops? On a retreat? To a monastery? To this last even Merton said "no." In his journal he wrote about the "fuss and ceremony," the "useless activity," and "the tensions of big functions" at Mass in Gethsemani. Little solitude was to be found there; it was a "non-existent" condition. Sometimes he remained alone in the silence of his hermitage "while everyone else says Mass."

I understood the valuable lesson Merton had learned in the middle of his life: "What matters is secret, not said. This begins to be the most real and the most certain dimension." Not from most books or in assigned prayers, certainly not in gatherings or retreats, and not with "the mumbling of lips," in Karl Barth's words in *On Prayer*, but from "the freedom of the heart" did I try to pray. The direction I thought I knew, the place I found, interior and solitary; which is to say that I was filled with contentment in the desert.

▦ THE TENSE FOR PRAYER: Merton said to "establish ourselves in the present." Let go of the past. Lose it forever; abandon concern about the future. Focus attention on NOW, on the moment. This was the English monk's thought: "You must fashion a cloud of forgetting beneath you, between you and every created thing." The eighteenth-century Jesuit Pierre de Caussade advised (Mark Gibbard in *the Study of Spirituality*) us that to "cut off all more distant views, we must confine ourselves to the duty of the present moment, without thinking of what preceded it or what will follow it."

How hard I found this. I think, I live, I act, I hurt, all in the present tense, but it was difficult to maintain that tense during prayer. The past pushed in mercilessly. Worry about the future nagged at me. Waiting in silence was a period that allowed concern for what might happen in the future to creep in. But I tried; often I failed.

▦ Whenever I began to think of myself as "a church of one," in Kathleen Norris's phrase in *The Cloister Walk*, I remembered her quotation from Martin Buber: "All [of us] have access to God, but each has a different access . . . the infinite multiplicity of the ways that lead to him, each of which is open to one [person]."

▓ I read Peter L. Berger's strong defense for the existence of established churches. Most of us, he said, "encounter transcendence (if at all) in an institutional setting of worship and instruction." He noted that "ecclesial belonging is a matter of 'vocation.'" This made room for such as me, for whom the vocation of belonging was frustrating, to be a solitary outsider. God works in strange ways, permitting an infinite number of itineraries on the way to Him.

▓ In his translation of Rainer Maria Rilke's *Letters* Stephen Mitchell said that "the ignorant think that God can be grasped by the mind; the wise know It is beyond knowledge." St. Paul called God's ways "unsearchable." Thomas Kelly in *Reality and the Spiritual World* was suspicious of "intellectual convincement of the reality of God" and saw it as far different from "the felt reality . . . the experience of Him."

I have been surprised to find that my lifelong reliance on the value of knowledge did not serve me in my search for God. I have read a great deal on the subject of prayer, and found much of value, as the number of quotations in this book will testify, but I had to scuttle most of it at the moment when I waited alone in prayer.

▓ From one of Merton's spiritual guides (in his *Journal*), Chuang Tzu: "Where can I find a man who has forgotten words? He is the one I would like to talk to."

I suspected Chuang Tzu might have met the man in silence, and listened closely to him if by chance the man had spoken, much as I have tried hard to learn to listen inwardly for a chance sound or sign of God. Thomas Kelly, in *Reality* . . . , warned against trying to bring young people to church by means of "a jitterbug program of fevered activities." Instead, he said, teach them how to listen, to *be quiet within themselves.* "For the listening to the eternal involves a silence within us." Silence is the best atmosphere for prayer, being undisturbed by talk and the effort of listening to others. We need little listening and less talk: "The closer God is, the less means are necessary" (Merton).

Further thoughts on writing. Henri Nouwen, talking about Merton in *Reaching Out,* said that for him writing was "a new experience of poverty. By his writing he had made himself and his most inner feelings and thoughts a public possession. In this way he had disowned himself and allowed others to enter his monastic silence." This is the grave danger of writing about prayer. It can be lost or at least buried in the published word, the way a file can disappear into the wilds of the hard disc if one makes a wrong stroke.

Meister Eckhart: "Only the hand that erases can write the true thing" (epigraph to Dag Hammarskjöld's *Markings*).

More on reading. In Alain de Botton's recent book, *How Proust Can Change Your Life,* I learned that Proust believed "Reading is on the threshold of the spiritual life; it can introduce us to it: it does not constitute it."

▨ In *The Cloister Walk* Norris declares she had no faith until "liturgy pulled me back." My faith grew stronger when I left liturgy behind and was pulled deeper into the privacy of silent and impromptu prayer.

Norris felt the Psalms could not be removed from a communal context. The Benedictines sing the Psalms because that practice "frees them from the tyranny of individual experience." I have read them silently in solitude without losing very much, I thought.

Norris quotes Gail Ramshaw's belief: "If we are agnostic much of the time, we can at least believe during the liturgy." And I, looking the other way, was in danger of unbelief until I found a way to pray alone.

Norris rediscovered her faith in church in the company of others: monks and oblates. I kept solitary company on the empty horizon of the cove. She went to a monastery; I moved into a private hermitage of prayer. Both ways were good, proof that the desire for the journey is what matters, not the path one takes, or even the hope of arrival.

▨ A C C I D I E. I had not heard that word since I learned years ago that it was used in medieval Latin to describe the sad state of some recluses who had fasted too much or practiced other means of self-punishment until they fell into prostration and despair. Later, I suppose, the simpler word "sloth" was substituted for it as a name for the fourth cardinal sin. Norris in *The Cloister Walk* told the story of a sick and elderly nun who asked a monk visiting her "if he thought that God had simply forgotten about her."

Hers was the accidie one feels inevitably in poor health and old age. It is the despair that afflicts the believer when she cannot find God, when she finds herself wondering why God has hidden His face. It is what Julian of Norwich said the Lord told her about inward prayer: "It does good, though you feel nothing, see nothing. Yes, even though you think you are doing nothing. For when you are dry, empty, sick, or weak, at such time is your prayer most pleasing to me though you find little enough to enjoy in it. This is true of all believing prayer."

Accidie: that old word, the inevitable result of God's continuing absence, the passionate desire for God's presence, the emptiness we must pass into and through on the way to Him.

▩ In my inquiry into the best prayer each morning (after the Psalms) I often wasted time trying out one word or another. That is, until I read in *The Cloister Walk* that Anthony, the fourth-century monk who lived in a desert fort, said that "the prayer of the monk is not perfect until he no longer realizes himself or the fact that he is praying."

▩ According to Michael Ivens in *The Study of Spirituality*, Ignatius Loyola, the sixteenth-century founder of the Jesuit Order, experienced the crucial moment in his spiritual journey on the bank of the Cardoner River. He called this supernatural event "an illumination" and "a great clarity" in his understanding. I was grateful to him for providing me with new vocabulary for my moment on the steps, although I knew that no words would ever seem exact enough, or ample enough, or in any way adequate.

▓ Again, on pain: From Marcel Proust, in Alain de Botton's fine account of his thought, I learned that the novelist suffered most of his life from a great number of illnesses. However, he believed pain had its use: "Infirmity alone makes us take notice and learn." We became more inquisitive, we think more when we suffer "because thinking helps us to put the pain in context. It helps us to understand its origins, plot its dimensions, and reconcile us to its presence." There is also the advantage that "suffering . . . opens up the *possibilities* for intelligent, imaginative inquiry." (These words are de Botton's paraphrase of Proust's observations in his great work *In Search of Lost Time*.)

▓ Again, the Psalms: Edward Kessler sent me an article taken from the Jesuit magazine *America*. It recounted the experience of the theologian Lawrence S. Cunningham praying the Psalms, in order, regularly, as I have been doing. I felt connected to Cunningham, as though he and I were a congregation, alone together, saying the same words but seated far apart, in different cities, he noting lines I had passed over. He was fond of "You have kept count of my tossings; / put my tears in your bottle" (56:8). In the King James Version, the Psalmist said to the Lord: "put tears into your bottle"; a slight difference but better poetry, we agreed.

I invited Thomas Merton into our gathering of two because Cunningham found it interesting that the monk said "he really learned the beauty of the Psalms when he said them under the pine trees far from the 'artifice' of a monastic choir."

▓ True religion is appetite, not history, fact, logic, custom, or reason. The Psalmist exhorted us to "taste and see that the Lord is good" (34:8), a startling instruction, until I remembered that the search for the experience of God was a hunger, a desire, a long meal with the promise of the reward of dessert after the first ineffable taste. Religion for many provided the taste of God, the Eucharist in memory of Him, not the sight, not the sound, but the appetite for God, in C. S. Lewis's phrase. Jacques Barzun, in his introduction to a late edition of William James's *The Varieties of Religious Experience,* said that James "will describe man's religious appetite" in his extraordinary book.

Speaking of Barzun, in the introduction I noticed that the celebrated critic was iconoclastic about both the saint and the parishioner. He called a saint "one-sided," for his life could not be a model for the rest of us, "and certainly not for the cowardly, spiritless churchgoer."

William James, in *The Varieties of Religious Experience,* wrote cautiously: "Religion shall mean for us the feelings, acts, and experiences of individual men in their solitude, so far as they apprehend themselves to stand in relation [to what] they may consider the divine." Note the careful, scholarly use of the ambiguous "to what they may consider."

I began to read *The Spiritual Life of Children* by Robert Coles. He quoted an early work by Sigmund Freud in which Freud considered that the "petty ceremonials" of any religion "can become tyrannical." Twenty years later he was even more harsh. Religion, he said, was filled with fairy tales, an illusion "derived from human wishes," a "consolation," and a response to "man's helplessness in the face of life's mysteries."

Coles, a psychiatrist, has written marvelously on the lives of children. He agrees with Freud's view about the history of religion. It was, he wrote, "mean-spirited, hate-filled, and all too ignorantly superstitious." It is, indeed, all of those things. And yet, the personal craving, the desire, the hunger for God persisted, long after the corrupt mess that "organized" religion often made on earth. Julian of Norwich observed that "by yearning for God we are made worthy." I think it was Perry Miller, authority on colonial history and literature, who pointed out that "Puritans spent their lives trying to hear God's voice."

My needs were singular and private, solitary and "quiet," a word an acquaintance used when she described the Quakerlike half hour she and a few other St. Brendan's parishioners in Stonington, Maine, held one evening a week. I was curious to know if she saw value in such gatherings over and beyond solitary, contemplative prayer. She said yes, "something" was present that she did not feel when she was alone.

Thomas Kelly, in *The Eternal Promise,* defined true Quaker group worship (what is called a "gathered meeting") as a special time

> when an electric hush and solemnity and depth of power steals over the worshipers. A blanket of divine covering comes over the room, a stillness that can be felt is over all, and the worshipers are gathered into a unity and synthesis of life that is amazing indeed. A quickening Presence pervades us, breaking down

some part of the special privacy and isolation of our individual
lives.

Such happenings depend (I imagine, since I have not experienced them) on the felt presence of a shared sense of the touch of
God, of "joint elevation," in Kelly's words.

My St. Brendan's acquaintance attended everything—Sunday
liturgy, Bible study classes, quiet-prayer groups. I asked her if she
had ever felt the presence of God in those places. She said yes,
many times, and under various conditions: before and after receiving communion, during her own private half hour of prayer,
in the quiet-prayer group.

I was disquieted by the thought of my long history of failure
to arrive at the yearned-for "experience" she had come to so
quickly. I wondered if I *had,* without being aware of it. Perhaps
the intensity of the moment on the steps had reduced all other encounters to insignificance.

Consolation from Thomas Kelly: "Mystics who are led deep
into the heart of devotion learn to be weaned away from reliance
upon special vision, learn not to clamor perpetually for the
heights but to walk in shadows and valleys and dry places for
months and years together."

▨ Add to definitions: Somewhere I read that Alfred North
Whitehead, philosopher and, with Bertrand Russell, author of a
famous book on mathematics, said, "Religion is what a man does
with his solitude."

▨ In my retreat into the interior I began to recognize how little
I seemed to need the trappings I once looked to as necessary for

worship. I found solace once again in Kelly's *The Eternal Promise:* "Christianity needs to get behind its still lingering confusion about the essential character of *any* external, even as beautiful as that of dramatizing the Lord's supper, and put first of all the sacrament of the heart, where God and man break bread together in the secret sanctuary of the soul." By stripping away the externals, by cleaning out the space wherein I prayed, like removing or covering the signs and symbols on the altar before Good Friday, was I trying to make room for the arrival of God?

▨ Question to myself: Was it disappointment after the fervor of a politically active youth that, in old age, turned me inward?

There were the few years during college when I worked at the Catholic Worker House on Mott Street in Greenwich Village in the company of other left-wing college students and a great woman, the Catholic activist Dorothy Day. She and her partner, Peter Maurin, with other young people, published *The Catholic Worker,* a newspaper full of strong antiwar sentiments, calls for assistance for the poor and the homeless, support for the rights of women prisoners. I was young and uncomfortably aware of my privileged position in New York life, indeed filled with guilt about it. I did not write for the paper; I felt honored to be asked to sell it, at a penny an issue, in Union Square.

Years later I served on a team of volunteers assisting in the care of AIDS patients in a hospital on Capitol Hill in Washington. We did minor tasks, like getting ice water, writing letters, making phone calls, and shopping for necessities. I was once sent to buy three pairs of jockey shorts for a young man with very specific requirements as to color, size, and texture. It took me an entire afternoon to accomplish this simple task.

But at other times being there was very hard. I witnessed tableaus of tragic rejection: parents who hovered at the doorway of their son's hospital room, afraid to enter or come close to him. I saw fury at the state of things when a sick young lawyer, denying the diagnosis made that evening, threw me out of the room when I offered help. "Help for *what?*" he screamed at me. I heard men, and one woman, in the throes of dying, cry out against what they knew was coming: "No." *No.*

Did that old passion to work for social betterment, egged on by disillusion with unchangeable humanity and the backward movement of progress, become inevitably, in old age, a search for God in His cloudy, indefinable, amorphous, hidden, and absent shape?

Is it the lost quiet in life in the world, buried under too much noisy humanity, too many buildings on every space, the effluvium, ringing, and clanging of billions of cars, trucks, planes, machines, boats, guns, elevators, and the uncounted products of modern technology, that has made me move into that place where silence can still be found, if I protect it from the outside? Could it be that, for me, as the English poet Elizabeth Jennings said at the end of her poem "Hermits and Poets," "what seemed like prayer was only concentration"?

▨ Yogi Berra (comic yet unknowingly wise pundit): "You can observe a lot by watching."

▨ I had found that writing about prayer diminished its effectiveness. But the other day, reading a review of Elizabeth Jennings's recent book of essays, I was encouraged to go on doing it.

Elizabeth Jennings wrote that Gerard Manley Hopkins "may say that God and experience of God are 'past telling of tongue,' but this does not prevent him from trying to tell these things and, what is more, from succeeding in doing so."

※ Add to thoughts on pain: Somewhere, Theophan, the Russian bishop and recluse, said, "The awareness of God shall be with you as clearly as a toothache."

※ Shortest instruction ever given on prayer: St. Paul advised the Thessalonians to "pray without ceasing" (1. 12:17).

※ Reading an autobiographical article in *The American Scholar,* I was appalled to learn that the characteristics of depression somewhat resemble my state when I was afflicted by shingles and when I prayed unavailingly. Was I, in each case, afflicted by deep depression?

Every case of depression, it seems, is unique, afflicting a unique individual, but there are some common symptoms. The author of the article, Joel P. Smith, asked for understanding of his reduced energy, totally absent enthusiasm for any project, profound, unending pessimism, and constant preoccupation with death. The four together created in him a terrible paralysis, physical and spiritual, a feeling of dread about the awful things that are surely to happen to him, and a fierce contempt for himself.

Smith's case, unlike William Styron's in *Darkness Visible* (Styron was severely depressed for only a few months), was lasting and not a matter of transient "blues" which we all suffer from at some time. So I was wrong to ally my blackness, failures, accidie, pessimism, and spiritual paralysis during contemplative prayer to his awful and continuing state.

The frightful thing about profound depression is that it cuts into the very core of the self. Smith wrote that "depression was in significant measure a spiritual affliction, our lives had lost meaning." This must be the darkest night of the mind and soul "when one's spiritual resources are used up."

We solitary seekers after a sense of God have felt a little of this at times. But we are saved, I believe, because our minds and spirits are not seriously ill, and only occasionally are we deserted by that strange, indescribable thing called faith.

Add to thoughts on seeking society: "Flee from creatures and hide yourself in God." —St. John of the Cross.

St. Benedict began his religious life as a hermit. He remained in that state for three years, living in a cave near a monastery until his disciples persuaded him to leave. He returned to the world to establish many monasteries, an interesting reversal of Thomas Merton's journey from the world to the monastery and then into further retreat, into his hermitage.

In *The New York Times* this year a good story: The Mother Superior of a Carmelite monastery was told by the Vatican, and her own bishop, to close it. The monastery was in Crown Heights, New York, a noisy place "not conducive to contemplation," the bishop said. But even if the monastery were to close, she wished to stay in that crowded, dangerous, noisy section of the city. She said that it was quite possible "to lead a little Carmelite life" in an apartment, for example, without the trouble the bureaucracy had brought upon her recently. "Meetings, meetings . . . I think the hierarchy is ruining religious life. I really believe you can return to the world and have your own place in secret."

This is similar to Merton's belief that modern-day persons could make use of the same contemplative prayer he was urging upon his fellows in Gethsemani, making us, in a way, monks in the world. It may be harder to pray alone without the walled-in protection against interruption that a monastery provided, but not impossible.

The longer I tried the fonder I became of the discipline it required. It represented a kind of victory over the forces of distraction and seduction in the world. For many, it was important to travel to a consecrated building in order to pray, to encounter God in some sense. But an apartment in a housing project in Crown Heights would serve the prayer purposes of the Carmelite Mother Superior. Add to this, in perhaps too absolute a statement, George Fox's belief (quoted by Thomas Kelly in *A Testament of Devotion*) that "God doesn't live in a house with a peaked roof. God lives inside people." For most believers, it must be said, the church or mosque or synagogue is precisely where God *does* reside.

I had begun to think that, like the very rich, God has many residences, many mansions, all of which contain the possibility that an avid visitor may, if he is very fortunate, find Him at home. St. Augustine believed in one of God's untraditional abodes: "He was within and we mistakingly sought Him without."

Blaise Pascal: "You would not seek me if you did not possess me."

The quietistic Archbishop Fénelon, responding to Descartes's *cogito, ergo sum*, was less sure of His exact location or even of the nature of His presence: "I am not what is. . . . I am almost what is not."

▨ Thomas Kelly, adding to my catalogue of using the senses to approach God: "Lead a *listening* life. Order your outward life so that nothing drowns out the listening."

▨ And, add sight. Robert Louis Stevenson, in *A Child's Garden of Verses:*

> If I could find a higher tree
> How much farther could I see.

Simone Weil: "Religion is nothing more than a looking."

▨ Add symbolic walking: At the beginning of this century, Rainer Maria Rilke wrote ten *Letters to a Young Poet* to instruct him in the practice of his craft, advice that might be applied as well to prayer: "Go into yourself [and] into your solitude" to discover if you are a true poet. "Keep growing, silently and earnestly" without ever looking outside. Do not "wait for outside answers to questions that only our innermost feeling, in your quietest hour, can perhaps answer."

And better: "What is necessary, after all, is only this solitude, vast inner inner solitude. To walk inside yourself and meet no one for hours—that is what you must be able to attain."

And the best: "Ask yourself, dear Mr. Kappus, whether you have really lost God. Isn't it more true to say that you have never yet possessed him?"

RETURN TO SIMONE WEIL

At the end of two years of reading I went back to *The Simone Weil Reader* because her wisdom, often condensed into one sentence, illuminated some dark moments for me. She put Elizabeth Jennings's definition of religion (as "concentration") into another form: "God is attention without distraction," an idea more process than discovery but still useful. She was too humble, too self-deprecating, to be able to believe in the Quaker concept of God within. She provided me with a fine sentence to add to my store of descriptions of Him: "We can only know one thing about God: that he is what we are not." The underlying assumption of her theology was always God's immeasurable distance from us and the pain we suffered at His remoteness: "God has left us abandoned in time," and "He stays far away from us, because if He approached us He would cause us to disappear."

I remembered the story of Jesus who was asked by a parent to heal his epileptic son (Mark 9:15). Jesus replied: "All things are possible to him who believes." The father said: "Lord, I believe." Then, strangely, he added: "Help thou my unbelief."

What about the order of these sentences? Reversed, they suggest an understandable progression. Or was it that the distraught father too hastily responded to Jesus to ensure the healing of his son, and then broke down in a fit of honesty in his second declaration? Ultimately, Weil declared, "The mysteries of the faith cannot be either affirmed or denied; they must be placed above that which we affirm or deny."

CODA

This people prays to me with their lips
but their heart is far from me.

—Isaiah, 29:13

FOR THE LIFE OF ME

The long siege of pain had almost lifted. It may have been that my body had exhausted its capacity to hurt, or, by means of the intensity of the pain, had almost cured itself. The childhood chicken pox virus retreated from the nerves, to be stored in tissues beyond sensation, leaving behind a small residue of feeling to remind me that until recently it had been in total command of all my time and senses. It was also possible that a course of treatments, in which a drug was topically applied and then sent down into the nerves by an electric current, had helped. The Pain Clinic's procedure was a sort of technological version of the laying on of hands.

Not once had I prayed for a cure, for if God was not attentive or present or even nearby, how could I ask Him for a favor? But prayer had served in other ways: it had distracted me from my body for very short periods of time. It had given me the transitory illusion of clear, inner emptiness from which the pain, like every other sensation, was absent. But when it asserted itself over the barriers of unknowing it presented me with the specter of mortality, goaded me into continuing my search.

Now, without my familiar, I was praying entirely alone. The cruel hand that had gripped my side for more than a year had almost withdrawn; the space around the area felt empty. To Julian of Norwich severe illness brought on "revelations," the wondrous appearance of the Lord Himself. For me, pain produced contradictory responses, at one time fury at the force that was a disturbing distraction, and at another, the rare opportunity to see everything more vividly, with a clarity I could only wonder at, in which the details of my present life were intensified and acutely delineated.

Marcel Proust knew this, and Don DeLillo as well, in his astonishing recent novel, *Underworld:* "Pain," he wrote, "is a form of information."

Shingles and its aftermath had been both affliction and gift, a salutary reminder of the approach of mortality ("Most things may never happen: this one will," in Philip Larkin's words), an intensification of the present moment. As for the future, I could not bear to think of it.

I returned to my hour of prayer free of the incubus that had clung to me for so long. At the time that its grip lessened, I had come to the end of my fourth cycle of Psalms. I started over again at Psalm 1 and, not surprisingly, with the clearer eye of near-painlessness, found myself stopping at new places, at lines of praise and gratitude for my release:

Happy are they all / who take refuge in him. (2:13)
You are my glory, the one who lifts up my head. (3:3)
You have put gladness in my heart. (4:7)
My heart is joyful because of your saving help. (13:5)

While I continued to notice the Psalmist's reproaches to God for His long silence and unexplained absence, I did not dwell on them as I had before. Even when I found that, as a parting gift, pain had left me with a precarious gait—I was as they say of the old "unsteady on my feet"—I accepted this *quid pro quo* as a lesson: I was forced, at long last, to sit still.

THE TIGER OF PEACE

Throughout my time of affliction I was grateful for many good tutors, a few for almost every sentence they wrote, others for a word or phrase here and there. For example, I came to realize how true was Anthony Bloom's description of prayer (in *Beginning to Pray*) as a "hard, arduous, daring exercise." If it succeeded, if one did manage to encounter God, one entered "the cave of a tiger—it is not a pussycat you meet—it is a tiger. The realm of God is dangerous."

I was reconciled to the terms of this image. I knew that I had not yet come near to God, pussycat or tiger, and that it was very possible I never would again. My expectation was not to encounter Him in any *form*, but rather as a *quality*, Something present, ineffable, nourishing. No longer did I hold out a hope for the sense of God as powerful and as memorable as the first experience. If the tiger never appeared, at least I began to understand that now, and for some time, and perhaps forever, I would be in the company of God's absence from me, consigned to His silence, sadly without the acute fever of direct encounter I had once known.

Real peace, what I felt while waiting in patience, in stillness and darkness, comforted and almost healed me: this was what I was beginning to know. I saw it as a reward of the journey. I should have paid attention to the English monk who spoke assuredly of his student that "finally there will come a moment when he experiences such peace and repose in that darkness that he thinks surely it must be God himself."

In that peace I thought I might have found an avatar of God, another form of that first sense of Him granted to me almost fifty years ago. Perhaps this was what It was, *all* It was, surely enough recompense for a long life and the long wait for Him. *My peace I give to you.* I hoped I would be able to settle for it, settle into it, finding His presence in His Absence, Something in His nothingness. "Yes . . . to the last it will remain *a cloud of unknowing* between him and his God," wrote the English monk.

If God's presence was always to be made manifest in nothingness, then it must be true that prayer itself was not a series of petitions or even a heartfelt string of thanksgivings, but a state of being, a nakedness of self in which I sat waiting in the climate of silence, imprisoned in a darkness from which there is no desire to escape. The Psalmist asked: "Where can I go then from your Spirit? / Where can I flee from your presence?" (139:6).

Somewhere I read a Wallace Stevens poem, in which he wrote that the "mind of winter" contemplated "nothing that is not there and nothing that is."

Walter told me of a hermit who lives less than forty miles away from me, sharing her life only with a sister on rare occasions. I wrote to her asking if we could meet so I could question her about prayer and solitude. I was satisfied by her non-response. It was entirely fitting and right that she never answered my letter.

SIGHTS

Two unknown (to the world) men floated up into my memory, both at first without significance to my thinking or in no logical context I could account for. They were unexpected arrivals on my motionless, contemplative journey.

Twenty years ago I went to midnight Mass in the beautiful

Ranchos de Taos church in New Mexico. As the service was starting, a very young Native American man with a heavily blanketed baby in his arms sat down beside me in the pew. He knelt at once and seemed to hold the baby up to the back of the pew in front of him as if he were directing his prayer to it or asking for something for it. Although there was room between us, he never put the bundle of sleeping baby down during the entire Mass, carrying it with him when he went to the rail for communion.

Then, when the rest of us returned to our seats, he made a short detour from the rail to the crêche at the side of the altar, knelt and held the child as close to the cradle of hay as he could. He said something I couldn't hear. I decided he was introducing his child to the one whose birthday we were celebrating, but no matter: whatever he said (or prayed), his posture before the crêche, his moving lips, and the light that shone in his brown eyes as he came back to the pew, was a moment to which I could only give the name "grace," an epiphany, a sight granted to an unworthy but grateful spectator.

The second encounter: One cold spring morning years ago I went to an early service in a Washington church within the close of the cathedral. I sat in my usual pew. A newcomer, a man whose age I could not guess, so covered was his face with beard and strands of long hair, came to the pew in front of me, moved to its end, and knelt. He wore a torn, knitted watch cap and a long, gray overcoat full of holes and without buttons. His shoes were remnants of colorless leather through which I could see the skin of his sockless feet.

The church was crowded, eight people in every pew. I watched as newcomers at the back spotted the one nearly empty pew and moved toward it, only to stop at the sight of the gray, kneeling vagrant and turn away to look for some other seat. Through the short liturgy he knelt there alone, a castaway on the only island in the church, his odor filling the space around him. He ignored the risings for the singing of hymns, the standing at the reading of the Gospel, the summons to the communion rail, so engrossed did he seem to be in his prayers.

I waited until the church was almost empty to see if he would leave with us, but when I reached the door he was still kneeling in the pew, a solitary, an *isolato*, left behind by prosperous parishioners and elegantly robed officials, needing none of us, sufficient unto himself, still absorbed in his prayers. I assumed (perhaps wrongly) that he was not acquainted with Merton's observation in *Contemplative Prayer:* "Once God has called you to solitude, everything you touch leads you further into solitude."

A friend told me that Flannery O'Connor had said, "Most of us come to the church by means the church does not allow."

THOU WHOM I DO NOT KNOW

The author of *The Cloud of Unknowing*, like Dionysius the Areopagite to whom he referred so often, was, in his tradition, called *apophatic.* They both concluded that God could be known only negatively, by what He was not. (William Johnson in his introduction to *The Cloud . . .* introduced me to this word.)

Many times as I prayed I held on to this idea, especially when writers on spiritual matters had informed me, with all the positive tones of certainty, what God thought, what He wanted of me, what His intentions were. The apophatic thought (like that of

Moses Maimonides, the twelfth-century mystic who believed that human reason could not reach God) was that we could know nothing about Him, especially what was in His mind. God was hidden, unable to be comprehended by any of the means human beings have available to their intellects.

Ignorance, in a way, was an advantage. It prevented me from making positive statements about God, or from expecting Him to present Himself to me because I was waiting for Him. Just as I could not believe that I was created in God's image (giving the ineffable a human shape), I knew I had to travel the *via negativa*, believing without evidence, with only the memory of the sense of evidence, the hardest kind of faith: "Lord, I believe. Help thou my unbelief."

BOULDING ON NAYLER

To those who wait without particular expectations, serendipitous and illuminating events may occur. During a visit to an old friend, I was shown a small book of sonnets by Kenneth Boulding, a poet I did not know. His twenty-six poems contained quotations from the deathbed words of a seventeenth-century Quaker, James Nayler, who was tortured and imprisoned for blasphemy. The first sonnet is titled with the first words of Nayler's: "There is a spirit which I feel." Another asks: "Are there no contraries at the heart of things?"

In the time that I had been thinking about prayer, and practicing it alone, my conviction grew that mine was *the* way, or, at the very least, the best way. Now I know that the contrary of my every assertion may be equally true. The unique pleasures I thought I had discovered could be regarded by many as egocentric and untrustworthy oddities. While I continued to live a monastic prayer life, I might well have failed to recognize the very real importance of communal worship: support for my efforts, comradeship with others engaged in a similar search, the warmth of church friendships and contacts, the unusual benefits of a "gathered meeting" in which more depth and insight might be achieved than one could manage alone.

The extremism of my choice, which left out all rite including the Eucharist, was entirely contrary to the customary acceptance of forms established by tradition. Was this a contrariness at the heart of things to be resolved by compromise? Should I move into the center on the theory that one did not cancel out the other, that both made the whole, supporting and throwing light on each other: two journeys, not one, to the same destination?

I have reexamined the dichotomy between finding God by means of service to others and the inactivity of solitary prayer. Having abandoned my youthful social action, working for those in the world who are in need or in trouble or who are unjustly treated, I may well have lost much of the humanity that once made me think that God was to be found and known in one's fellow men and women. Boulding wrote: "So I have tried / to wall out God with deeds. / And yet inside my soul blazes His light, despite my screen."

Are there no contraries at the heart of things?

MISSING WORDS

When I looked back through these pages I noted that words usually found in writings about prayer were largely absent—*soul, spiritual* and *spirituality, immortality, Jesus, heaven, hell, hope, love, sin, Christian* and *Christianity.*

These are all highly connotative nouns, words with strong histories around which my life of faith had been built. It surprised me to see how far from these customary verbal choices I had moved: solid-seeming nouns had given way to tentative adjectives and gerunds, almost all suggesting the present tense—*waiting, searching, listening, hurting, absent, solitary.*

I had fallen into a kind of reductionism, passing over the richness of connotation, simplifying vocabulary until what remained centered around one word: *God;* and then settled for even less: *the sense of God.*

I thought of Thomas Merton quoting the *Ecrits Spirituels* of Father Monchanin, in which one of my missing words appears: "Now is the hour of the garden and the night, the hour of silent offering: *therefore the hour of hope:* God alone. Faceless, unknown, unfelt, yet undeniable: God."

BEASTS IN THE JUNGLE

My daughter, Barbara Wheeler, has been actively involved in church matters all her adult life. She is a much-in-demand lecturer and homilist, a scholar and collaborative author of books on congregational life and the formative nature of seminary education. We talked recently about dangers she saw inherent in my manner of prayer. The beasts in the solitary jungle through which I have continued to walk are spiritual oddity and growing eccentricity. Without a community of worshipers, sustaining each other's faith and serving Christ's injunctions about service to the world in His name, I may fall (may have already fallen) into narcissism, sterile exercises of the mind, idiosyncratic, even mistaken and arid ways of searching for God.

To act, she said, was essential to worship, a sign of faith, a signal to the rest of the world of one's commitment to God. She shared the general view that "not what we think, but what we do has been / the standard of the world" (Boulding once more).

The strongest argument she made against my practice was this: private prayer is very hard. Indeed, it may be impossible to sustain it for any length of time. Most human beings have not the stamina or the strength of will to carry it on alone for very long. But participating with others regularly in prescribed ritual has a very good chance of keeping alive one's prayer life, perhaps even one's faith.

I have no answer to this, having done what I am doing for less than three years, not long enough to apply the endurance test to it. I may never have to learn the answer because the time remaining to me is limited. But while it lasts, contemplative prayer continues to absorb me: it has refreshed my faith. I believe I have found out something about the proper posture ("proper," remember, for me alone, not for everyone, not for those contented with where they are now) in which to wait, something about the spiritual rewards of the Psalter I have chosen to pray, a little about expressing gratitude to *Whose I am* for granting me the place and the clement climate of seclusion, silence, and solitude for prayer. It would be fine to think that all I have been granted thus far will last as long as I do.

But there is grave danger, I know well, in being proud of my practice, of what I have learned and done in this time. Pride is the uncritical approval of the self, hauteur at the pleasure and contentment of being alone much of the time, an egotistic presumption that my waiting will someday be rewarded. It is the arrogance of being contented to be alone while I wait. It is as if the solitary self is somehow too good to ask the world for assistance. Again I read Kenneth Boulding's words: "Ah, Lord, run through me with thy sudden tide, / for this proud heart can never be Thy throne / unless its pride be pride of Thee alone."

KEEPING COMPANY

I often think of Simone Weil. Her *Spiritual Autobiography* describes her two extraordinary experiences of God for which she was entirely unprepared, never having prayed, never having attended a synagogue or a church: "I may say that never in my life have I 'sought for God.' " But still, He came to her. After those surprising times she made what she called "spiritual progress" by working in factories and laboring in fields, starving herself in order to share the lives of the poor. For many years this was her only form of prayer. "I never said any words to God, either out loud or mentally," she wrote, until she came upon the Our Father while studying Greek. She fell in love with the prayer and said it many times a day for the rest of her short life.

To her Christ and His Father were inseparable: "I was incapable of thinking of him without thinking of God."

She lived on the edge of a church she believed in, but never joined, feeling unworthy, "a castaway" object, fit only to be rejected by God, a representative of all those who had faith while remaining on the threshold of established religion. She knew God in Christ's words: "Thy Father who seeth in secret." She wrote, "The word of God is the secret word."

Dag Hammarskjöld quoted the saying of the thirteenth-century Sufi master Jalal-ad-Din Rumi. In one way, it describes Simone Weil: "The lovers of God have no religion but God alone."

To me, Weil's was an admirable if sometimes eccentric life, full of pain, unexpected "experiences" of God, strong and active alliances with the despised of the earth, the practice of taking prayer from poetry.

When I think about her, and about my own life of prayer, I remember the words of the Talmud:

> Look ahead.
> You are not expected to complete the task.
> Neither are you permitted to lay it down.

BIBLIOGRAPHY

I have drawn heavily, and quoted often, from the following books:

Anon. *The Cloud of Unknowing.* New York: Image Books/Doubleday, 1973.

Berger, Peter L. *A Far Glory.* New York: The Free Press, 1992.

Bloom, Anthony. *Beginning to Pray.* New York: Paulist Press, 1970.

Bonhoeffer, Dietrich. *Life Together.* HarperSanFrancisco, 1954.

Coles, Robert. *The Spiritual Life of Children.* Boston: Houghton Mifflin, 1990.

The Collected Works of St. John of the Cross. Washington, D.C.: ICS Publications, 1991.

Eckhart, Meister. *The Essential Sermons, etc.* New York: Paulist Press, 1981.

Furlong, Monica. *Travelling In.* London: Hodder & Stoughton, 1971.

Hammarskjöld, Dag. *Markings.* New York: Alfred A. Knopf, 1965.

Hillman, James. *Kinds of Power.* New York: Doubleday, 1995.

James, William. *The Varieties of Religious Experience.* New

York: Modern Library, n.d. (Published originally in 1902.)

Julian of Norwich. *Revelations of Divine Love.* New York: Penguin Books, 1996.

Kazantzakis, Nikos. *The Saviors of God: Spiritual Exercises.* New York: Touchstone/Simon & Schuster, 1969.

Kelly, Thomas. *Reality and the Spiritual World.* Philadelphia: Pendlehill Books, 1942.

———. *The Eternal Promise.* Richmond, Ind.: Friends United Press, 1988.

———. *A Testament of Devotion.* HarperSanFrancisco, 1996.

The Literary Guide to the Bible. Cambridge, Mass.: Harvard University Press, 1986. Edited by Robert Alter and Frank Kermode.

Luther, Martin. *Works,* Vol. 42. Philadelphia: Fortress Press, 1969.

Merton, Thomas. *Seeds of Contemplation.* New York: New Directions, 1949.

———. *Zen and the Birds of Appetite.* New York: New Directions, 1968.

———. *Contemplative Prayer.* New York: Image Books/Doubleday, 1990.

———. *Turning Toward the World.* The Journals, Vol. 4. HarperSanFrancisco, 1996. Edited by Victor A. Kramer.

Norris, Kathleen. *Dakota.* Boston: Houghton Mifflin, 1993.

———. *The Cloister Walk.* New York: Riverhead Books, 1996.

Nouwen, Henri J. M. *Reaching Out.* New York: Doubleday, 1975.

The Study of Spirituality. New York: Oxford University Press, 1986. Edited by Cheslyn Jones, Geoffrey Wainwright,

and Edward Yarnold, S.J. This volume has served me
well as a valuable source of information and guide to
further reading.

Weil, Simone. *Waiting for God*. New York: G. P. Putnam's Sons,
1951. Introduction by Leslie A. Fiedler.

The Simone Weil Reader. New York: David McKay, 1977. Edited
by George A. Panichas.

The poem "Love" is from George Herbert's *The Temple*, found in
many editions and anthologies. I have quoted from *The Complete Poems of Emily Dickinson*, edited by Thomas H. Johnson
(Boston: Little, Brown, 1960); Philip Larkin, *Collected Poems*,
edited by Anthony Thwaite (New York: Farrar, Straus and Gi-
roux, 1989); Alfred Lord Byron, *Don Juan*, written in 1819 and
found in all collections of his works as well as in anthologies;
Poems of Gerard Manley Hopkins (London: University Press,
1918); and Dag Hammarskjöld, *Markings*, cited above.

I have referred to Hyder Rollins's edition of *The Letters of John
Keats*, Vol. 1, published by Harvard University Press in 1958; the
fiction of William Miller, *A Canticle for Leibowitz* (New York:
Lippincott, 1939); and Fyodor Dostoevsky's *Crime and Punishment* and J. D. Salinger's *Franny and Zooey*, both of which appear
in many editions. The references to Marcel Proust's views on
pain come from Alain de Botton's *How Proust Can Change Your
Life*, published in 1997 by Pantheon.

The biography *The Knox Brothers* by Penelope Fitzgerald was
published by Coward, McCann & Geoghegan in 1977. The article on depression is from *The American Scholar* (Autumn 1997).
Quotations from the work of Elizabeth Jennings were taken from
a review of her work by Clive Wilmer in the *Times Literary Sup-*

plement (August 1997). Lawrence Cunningham wrote on "Praying the Psalms" in *America* (August 2, 1997). Stephen Mitchell translated Rainer Maria Rilke's *Letters to a Young Poet,* published by Random House in 1983. Kenneth Boulding's *The Nayler Sonnets* were published by Fellowship Publications in New York in 1945. I have found some interesting quotations in *The Temple in the House* (New York: Putnam, 1994) by Anthony Lawler.

Throughout I have used the Revised Standard Version of the Psalms found in *The Book of Common Prayer,* which I find comfortable and often linguistically more attractive. It is always at hand for me when I wish to pray. Kathleen Norris's commentary on and edition of the King James Version arrived too late for me to consult.

AUTHOR'S NOTE

All through this book I see I have used the
traditional and no longer politically correct
pronoun for God, perhaps because of long, in-
grained habit, but *not* because I have a fixed
idea of God's gender. The word "God" grows
tedious and unfelicitous when it appears two
or three times in a sentence or paragraph; so I
have used the masculine pronoun for, I fear,
literary reasons.